MW01715195

THE SHAAR PRESS

THE JUDAICA IMPRINT FOR THOUGHTFUL PEOPLE

A psychiatrist finds a wealth of ideas in the weekly Torah reading

THE SHAAR PRESS

Windows to the Soul

ויקרא - במדבר - דברים

LEVITICUS – NUMBERS – DEUTERONOMY

Rabbi Michael Bernstein, M.D.

First edition – First impression / March 2001

Published by **SHAAR PRESS**
Distributed by MESORAH PUBLICATIONS, LTD.
4401 Second Avenue / Brooklyn, N.Y 11232 / (718) 921-9000

Distributed in Israel by SIFRIATI / A. GITLER
6 Hayarkon Street / Bnei Brak 51127

Distributed in Europe by LEHMANNS
Unit E, Viking Industrial Park, Rolling Mill Road / Jarrow, Tyne and Wear, NE32 3DP/ England

Distributed in Australia and New Zealand by GOLDS WORLD OF JUDAICA
3-13 William Street / Balaclava, Melbourne 3183 / Victoria Australia

Distributed in South Africa by KOLLEL BOOKSHOP
Shop 8A Norwood Hypermarket / Norwood 2196, Johannesburg, South Africa

ISBN: 1-57819-493-8 Hard Cover
ISBN: 1-57819-494-6 Paperback

Printed in the United States of America by Noble Book Press
Custom bound by Sefercraft, Inc. / 4401 Second Avenue / Brooklyn N.Y. 11232

This volume is dedicated to the memory of

My father-in-law

אברהם מרדכי בן מאיר שלמה ע"ה

Abram Baum ע"ה

A man of exceptional honesty, intellect and kindness,

he rose from among the ashes of Aushwitz to build a family,

but his life was cut short before he could enjoy
his many grandchildren.

לעילוי נשמת

חיים נתן בן נפתלי צבי ע״ה

Neil Blond ע״ה

Neil was a dear friend, remarkable for his brilliance, *joie de vivre*, humor, kindness, and integrity.

His presence is greatly missed by all who were close to him.

Rabbi CHAIM P. SCHEINBERG
Rosh Hayeshiva "TORAH ORE"
and Morah Hora'ah of Kiryat Mattersdorf

הרב חיים פינחס שיינברג
ראש ישיבת ״תורה אור״
ומורה הוראה דקרית מטרסדורף

מכתב ברכה

י״ח אייר, תש״ס

הנה שלחו לפני את ספרו של הר״ר מיכאל ברנשטיין נ״י רופא מומחה בפסיכיאטריה. מחמת טרדותי הרבות ומאפס הפנאי לא יכולת לעיין בדבריו, אבל נמסר לי על ידי אחד מתלמידי החשובים שליט״א על גודל מסירותו של המחבר ללימוד ושקידת התורה. וגם שמעתי שרבנים חשובים שליט״א שיבחו את הספר שניכר מתוך דבריו גודל יגיעו ועמלו בהכנת המקרא. על כן אמרתי, אף שאינני נותן הסכמות על ספרים מטעמים כמוסים עימדי, מ״מ הנני מברכו שיהיה ספרו לתועלת הרבים לקרבם לתורה ולתעודה, ובפרט לאחינו שעודם רחוקים מדרך התורה, ויזכה המחבר להמשיך להגדיל תורה ולהאדירה מתוך מנוחת הנפש והרחבת הדעת.

חיים פינחס שיינברג

הכותב וחותם לכבוד התורה ולומדיה
חיים פנחס שיינברג

דוד קאהן

ביהמ״ד גבול יעבץ
ברוקלין, נוא יארק

בס״ד

כבוד הרב המאור הגדול ר׳ מיכאל דר. ברנשטיין שליט״א

I have perused many chapters of your sefer and was impressed by its depth and originality as well as the clarity with which your ideas are presented.

Fortunate is the one who uses his innate and developed talents in the service of G-d. You, indeed, have the great merit of disseminating Torah thoughts by using your originality and your psychological perception to plumb the depths of the Torah.

אשריך ואשרי חלקך

דוד קאהן
רב דביהמ״ד גבול יעבץ
כ״ג תמוז תש״ס

בס"ד

מתתיהו
matityahu

הרב זאב לף
מרא דאתרא מושב מתתיהו
ראש הישיבה ישיבה גדולה מתתיהו
ד.נ. מודיעין 71917
טל 08-976-1138 פקס. 08-976 5326

RABBI ZEV LEFF
Rav of Moshav Matityahu
Rosh Hayeshiva
Yeshiva Gedola Matisyahu
D.N. Modiin 71917 Israel
08-976-1138 Fax 08-976-5326

Tammuz 29,5760

I have had the pleasure to read a portion of the manuscript of "Windows to the Soul" by Dr. Michael Bernstein נ"י. I found the material presented refreshing and interesting, informative, thought provoking, and inspiring.

Dr. Bernstein presents many new ideas in explaining various Torah topics, and although innovative I have found them to be well rooted in Torah sources and reflecting a true Torah perspective. I have found many lessons in Torah practice and thought that can be culled from these Divrei Torah. Additionally the author's professional experience as a child psychologist is woven into the Torah insights that truly present windows to the soul.

Although I had the opportunity to see the material only on Sefer Bereshis in its entirety and portions of Sefer Shmos, I am confident based on the integrity of the author and the solid consistency of the Divrei Torah I read ,that all the Sedras are dealt with in a like manner.

I highly recommend this Sefer as a source of serious Torah learning and as a resource for family discussion to enhance the Shabbos table,להגדיל תורה ולהאדירה

With Torah blessings,

Zev Leff

Rabbi Zev Leff
Moshav Matityahu

Table of Contents

The Book of Leviticus / Vayikra

The Book of Numbers / Bamidbar

ויקרא
LEVITICUS

פרשת ויקרא
Parashas Vayikra

The Second Pillar of Creation

CREATION RESTS ON A TRIPOD. THE ENTIRE WORLD, according to our Sages (*Avos* 1:2), is supported by three pillars — Torah, *avodah* and acts of kindness — and should one of them be removed, the entire edifice would collapse. *Avodah*, the second pillar of creation, refers to the Divine service performed by the Kohanim, the priestly caste, in the *Mishkan* and, afterwards, in the Temple; this is the overarching theme of the Book of Leviticus. Tragically, the Divine service has been interrupted for some two thousand years, ever since the destruction of the Second Temple. In the absence of the second pillar, how is creation supported?

There is a substitute. The prophet declares (*Hosea* 14:3), "*U'neshalmah farim sefaseinu*. We will supply bullocks with our lips." In other words, prayer can take the place of the interrupted

Divine service. Moreover, the Talmud (*Berachos* 26b) correlates the three daily prayers to the three primary offerings of the Temple service.

How does prayer serve as a surrogate Divine service? After all, prayer is essentially a personal act of reflection, introspection and self-criticism. It is the silent, inwardly directed "duty of the heart," whereas the Divine service is an elaborate and demonstrative set of physical acts performed as homage to God. How do we bridge the chasm between prayer and Divine service? Why is prayer, more than any other commandment, the surrogate for the Divine service?

As expressed in the Torah, God's goal is to create a realm on earth where His presence is manifest and thereby extend His Divinely willed good to all mankind. Thus, there is a duality in all the commandments. They are personal acts that draw us closer to God as individuals, and also serve collectively as an expression of the servitude of the Jewish nation to God. This second sacred duty endows the performance or nonperformance of every mitzvah with the potential of a sanctification or desecration of His Name.

Most of the mitzvos address the idea of personal perfection either indirectly or by addressing a specific character trait. For instance, a person who performs a mitzvah commemorating a certain important historical event is creating and solidifying a personal bond with God, which elevates and perfects him; it is the resulting relationship more than the act itself that elevates his existence. Two mitzvos, however, are pure acts of human perfection — prayer and Torah study.

Of these two, prayer more directly addresses personal improvement through human emotion; it is the supreme deliberate attempt to bring the human personality ever closer to its perfect form. It follows that for the Jewish people collectively prayer is the most effective way to express our servitude and heighten the awareness of God's presence among men. In this sense, prayer takes the place of the Divine service; we perfect ourselves as members of a nation whose collective duty is to reveal God's presence, and this endeavor to achieve self-perfection (*sh'leimus*) is in itself our service of God.

In this light, we gain new insight into the *Shema*. The Talmud (*Berachos* 63b) states that if a person deliberately neglects to say the obligatory *Shema* even once, it is as if he has never said it. Why so harsh a judgment?

The *Shema* is a declaration of faith and acceptance of the obligation to serve God (*kabbalas ohl Malchus Shamayim*). It cumulatively transforms a person and brings him ever closer to God. Each day, as he draws closer, the possibility of a deliberate omission becomes ever more remote. Therefore, if a person deliberately neglects the *Shema*, it proves he has never really said it properly, that it was never more than lip service.

During the *Amidah* of the festivals, we say, "You chose us from among all the people, You loved us and favored us. You lifted us above all the polyglot nations and sanctified us with Your commandments. You drew us close, our King, to Your service, and proclaimed Your great and holy Name over us."

Only on the festivals do we speak about being "lifted above all the polyglot nations," making reference both in the *Amidah* and in the *Kiddush* to the superiority of Hebrew over the myriad languages of the world. There is no such mention in the Sabbath liturgy. What is the connection between the Hebrew language and the festivals?

Both the Sabbath and the festivals are sanctified, but they differ. The sanctity of the Sabbath is inherent, and it is our obligation to acknowledge it. We do not create its sanctity. We are, however, involved in creating the sanctity of the festivals. We do it indirectly by declaring the new months and establishing the calendar dates; we bless God "Who sanctifies Israel and the times," which the Sages interpret as "Who sanctifies Israel who in turn sanctify the times." We also do it directly by the special festival offerings in the Temple.

After the destruction of the Temple, we no longer have the ability to bring the festival offerings, but we do have a substitute.

Through our prayers, it is considered as if we brought the appropriate sacrifices, and in this way, we continue to participate in the sanctification of the festivals. Therefore, the Hebrew language, perfectly constructed and nuanced for holiness, plays a major role in the festival observance and earns special mention in their liturgical prayers.

Symmetry and elegance pervade God's creation. We find one example of this harmony in the three pillars of the world. *Nefesh HaChaim*, among many Kabbalistic works, identifies the lower three elements of the human soul as *nefesh*, *ruach* and *neshamah*. They correlate respectively with man's physical self and actions, his emotional states and his intellectual activity.

Man's task is to improve these aspects of the soul. Fittingly, the Torah obliges us to place *tefillin* on our arms, near our hearts and near our brains, the three parts of the body associated with the three levels of the soul.

As we consider the three pillars identified by our Sages, we may discern the quintessential ideals of these three levels — kindness, service and prayer, and Torah study. As man struggles and prevails in these areas, he ennobles these aspects of his soul and thereby strengthens the pillars of creation.

פרשת צו
Parashas Tzav

The Center Point of the Torah

S*OFRIM*, LITERALLY "COUNTERS," IS THE NAME THE TALMUD (*Kiddushin* 30a) gives to the first generations of rabbis after the age of prophecy came to an end. These rabbis "counted" every verse, word and letter of the Torah.

They determined that the middle verse of the Torah is right here in *Parashas Tzav* (8:8): "[Moses] placed the breastplate upon him [Aaron]; and he put the *Urim VeTumim* into the breastplate"; that the middle words are *darosh darash* (10:16); and that the letter *vav* in the word *gachon* (11:42), belly, is the middle letter of the Torah (according to the Masoretic tradition, the *vav* is written larger than the others).

All three "middles" suggest a symbolic progression. The letter *vav* means "and" or "hook," connecting the two halves of the Torah. Letters build into words, and the middle two words, *darosh darash*, which mean "thoroughly investigate," encourage investigation of these two halves. Finally, the goal of our learning expresses itself in the Kohen Gadol's breastplate, the conduit of connection between God and man through which we receive direct communication.

Regardless of the significance we assign to the identified "middles," there remains a delineation of the Torah into halves. What is the significance of this division into halves? We understand the division of the Torah into five Books, since each has its own respective theme. But why did the early rabbis seek the Torah's middle point? Where do we find a difference between the Torah's first half and its second?

In considering the cycles of the Jewish calendar, the *Zohar* refers to the first half of the year, starting in the spring month of Nissan, as a reflection of *is'arusa di'le'eila* (stimulus from Above), and to the second half, starting in the autumn month of Tishrei, as a reflection of *is'arusa di'le'satta* (self-generated stimulus).

The *Zohar* sees the first two festivals of the year, Passover and Shavuos, as more passive, commemorating God's actions in taking us out of Egypt and giving us the Torah. During these months, we also commemorate Tishah B'Av, grieving for the losses we have endured throughout our history. The second half of the year, however, reflects our more active involvement. On Rosh Hashanah, we acknowledge God's kingship; we also inaugurate a period of introspection and repentance that reaches its climax on Yom Kippur. On Succos, we leave our homes and live in a *succah* to commemorate the forty years we spent in the desert studying Torah. Chanukah and Purim, which also fall during this time, commemorate the providential victories of the Jewish people in the face of spiritual and physical peril.

The progressive development of the text of the Torah seems to follow this pattern. The first half of the Torah tells of God's creation, His providential acts, such as the Flood, His selection of Abraham, the formation and redemption of the Jewish people, the giving of the Torah and the instructions for building the *Mishkan*. The participation of the Jewish people is more passive;

it is a text of *is'arusa di'le'eila*, stimulus from Above. In the second half of the Torah, the Jewish people are more active — sometimes to their credit, sometimes not — as the theme shifts to *is'arusa di'le'satta*, man's own awakening. We encounter the nation's first failed attempt to scout out and conquer the Promised Land, the rebellion of Korach, the wars against Og and Sichon, the final march to the doorstep of Israel and Moses' own ethical exhortations to the Jewish people for the entire length of the Book of Deuteronomy.

In a certain sense, this cycle from the passive to the active mirrors the developmental transition of human life. An infant is helpless; he needs to be fed, bathed and sheltered. A child is not quite as helpless but still requires nurturance for his intellectual and moral development as well as training in the skills that will help him earn a livelihood. Later, when he moves into the mature stage of life, he can become an active giver and doer.

If we look more closely, we can also discern a foreshadowing of the general course of Jewish history in the pattern of the Jewish calendar year. All events since the first conquest of Canaan fall into three successive epochs: the First Temple Era that ended with Babylonian destruction; the Second Temple Era that ended with the Roman destruction; and the Third Temple Era to which our present 2,000-year exile is a prelude.

Our Sages have identified the causes for the demise of the First Temple as the sins of idolatry, adultery and murder, all associated with man's most primitive animalistic drives (*nefesh habahami*). In a sense, we may consider the festival of Passover a correction (*tikkun*) for these impulses. Our Sages viewed *chametz* as a representation of the *se'or she'b'issah*, "the leaven in the dough," that symbolizes man's general *yetzer hara* (evil inclination). They considered eating the unleavened matzah and the paschal lamb as a symbolic reversal of man's instinctual appetitive desire. Moreover, the lamb represents the Egyptians' deities, and its slaughter expresses our rejection of pagan idolatrous practices. A theme emerges in the first festival of the year: Man brings his instinctual forces under the dominion of his higher self in God's service.

The sin of baseless hatred (*sinas chinam*), according to our Sages, caused the destruction of the Second Temple. During the Second Temple period, Torah scholarship flourished, but this effulgence did not sufficiently integrate itself into the personalities of the scholars to avoid a second destruction and exile. This period, in the grand scheme of history, correlates with the second festival of Shavuos, which celebrates our receiving of the Torah.

The final Temple awaits the Messianic era, which corresponds to the festival of Succos. God states (*Exodus* 25:8), "Build Me a *Mishkan*, and I will dwell amongst them." On Succos, each Jew dwells in his temporary structure, which recalls the clouds of glory that followed the Jewish people in the desert; his home becomes a miniature tabernacle reminding him of God's presence and providence. Our Sages relate the idealized dwelling of the Succos holiday to the Third Temple epoch; for example, during Succos, we petition God at the end of *Birchas HaMazon* for the restoration of "King David's fallen *succah*," which refers to the Temple.

The addition of the rabbinic festivals solidifies the association between the flow of the Jewish year and all of Jewish history. Chanukah, which falls during the darkest time of the year, is a festival of light celebrating our resistance to the dark period of Greek assimilation. Purim occurs at the end of the year; it celebrates our victory over Haman the Amalekite. At the end of history, our victory over Amalek, the sworn enemies of God and His people, will usher in the Messianic era.

What benefit is there in all this foreshadowing? It prepares us for the future by familiarizing us with its forms and structures and ensuring that the psychological impact will be profound. As we, the Jewish people, plod through history, we are already well acquainted with the template of history's ultimate unfolding and successful resolution. Our yearly cycle infuses us, on both the conscious and unconscious level, with a hope and confidence that our long exile will reach its successful conclusion.

The Talmud (*Rosh Hashanah* 11a) records a dispute between Rabbi Eliezer and Rabbi Yehoshua as to the exact date of creation. According to Rabbi Eliezer, creation occurred on the 25th of Elul, and Adam was born six days later on the first of Tishrei, which is Rosh Hashanah. According to Rabbi Yehoshua, creation occurred on the 25th of Adar, and God created Adam on the first of Nissan.

The Ran questions why, according to Rabbi Yehoshua, God established the day of judgment on the first of Tishrei. If no significant event of creation took place on that day, why did God invest it with such solemnity?

The Ran finds a solution in the proximity of Rosh Hashanah to Yom Kippur, the ultimate day of forgiveness, which occurs on the 10th of Tishrei, the day God forgave the Jewish people for making the Golden Calf. God fixed Rosh Hashanah, the Day of Judgment, ten days earlier in order to put people into the right frame of mind for atonement.

Perhaps we can add yet another thought. The first of Tishrei stands at the cusp of the second half of the year, at the starting point of the *is'arusa di'le'satta*, man's own awakening, described by the *Zohar*. This is the time most propitious for self-examination, self-improvement and self-redemption. This is when God judges man to determine if he will "awaken" to fulfill God's will.

פרשת שמיני
Parashas Shemini

i. Waiting for Love

THE INAUGURATION OF THE *MISHKAN* WAS COMPLETED ON Rosh Chodesh, the Festival of the New Moon, which takes place on the first day of the new month. According to the Midrash (*Tanchuma*), this timing reflects the importance Rosh Chodesh plays in Jewish life and thought. What specifically connects these two events?

Rosh Chodesh was the first commandment God gave the Jewish people collectively. The Midrash sees the moon as the quintessential symbol of the Jewish people whose fortunes periodically wane only to wax full again. Furthermore, the Jewish people reflect the glory of God, much as the moon reflects the sunlight.

When the Sabbath falls on the eve of Rosh Chodesh, we read a special *Haftarah* from the Book of Samuel (20:14-42). It tells of Jonathan, King Saul's son, and his friend David, the brilliant courtier who incurs Saul's disfavor through no fault of his own.

Saul is violently jealous of David, and Jonathan fears his father may kill his beloved friend.

Jonathan arranges to send David a signal should it become necessary for him to flee. They make their plans the day before Rosh Chodesh. There is to be a royal feast the next day in honor of Rosh Chodesh, and Jonathan will gauge his father's feelings toward David, whose seat will be empty. Afterward, Jonathan will come to a field as if to practice his archery, while David is to hide in the bushes. They arrange a signal. If Jonathan overshoots the mark, David will know to stay away. If he undershoots, David will know he may return safely. In the end, Jonathan overshoots the mark, then sends his attendant away. The friends embrace and bid each other farewell.

Why did our Sages select this *Haftarah* for the Sabbath on the eve of Rosh Chodesh? Is it because of the incidental mention of a Rosh Chodesh feast the following day? It is unlikely that the connection is so tenuous.

This observation leads to an even more fundamental question. Why did our Sages find it necessary to select a special *Haftarah* for a Sabbath that falls on the day before Rosh Chodesh? The *Haftarah* usually relates to a theme of the *parashah*, unless a special occasion coincides with the Sabbath and preempts the regular *Haftarah*. Why is the eve of Rosh Chodesh such a special occasion?

Let us take a closer look at the story itself. An obvious question presents itself. If it was possible all along for Jonathan to send off his attendant and meet with David directly, why devise the elaborate system of arrow signals? Why didn't they simply arrange to meet, as in fact they did?

Apparently, Jonathan changed his mind after making the arrangement. There was a significant element of risk in a meeting with the fugitive David, and originally, Jonathan did not consider it worth taking. Better to play it safe. But the events of the previous night convinced him that the situation was worse than he had imagined; the rift was irreparable. What changed Jonathan's mind?

When King Saul noticed David's empty seat, he became so enraged he wanted to kill his own son Jonathan, whom he blamed for David's flight. This was a revelation to Jonathan. He had assumed his father's antagonism arose from an understandable concern about David as a contender for the throne. But how could such antagonism vent itself by killing Jonathan, the very heir to the throne whose rights Saul was ostensibly protecting? If Saul was prepared to kill his own son Jonathan, it was clear proof that his was a hopelessly irrational rage that would not abate with the mere passage of time. Jonathan now knew that reconciliation between David and Saul was impossible.

With this sad realization, Jonathan felt he had to risk a meeting with his beloved friend to bid him a final farewell. Their last words to each other are an expression of transcendent love. Our Sages considered (*Avos* 5:19) theirs the paradigm of pure love, a love deriving from the mutual recognition of the other's eternal virtues.

This love finds an echo in the new month, which reflects God's eternal relationship with and love for the Jewish people. Anticipation is an expression of love, and fittingly, the observance of Rosh Chodesh already goes into force one day earlier, when the court, as the representative body of the Jewish people, anticipates the new moon, seeking out witnesses who can testify to its presence. In this sense, the day before Rosh Chodesh is already a special occasion and deserves its own *Haftarah*. The *Haftarah* chosen focuses on the virtuous love and devotion between David and Jonathan, a metaphor for the love between God and the Jewish people, a love reflected in the institution of Rosh Chodesh.

The inauguration of the *Mishkan* initiated a twelve-day celebration filled with anticipation, and bursting with the love of the Jewish people for God. Appropriately, it began on Rosh Chodesh.

ii. A Miniature Temple

KOHANIM AND THEIR DUTIES DOMINATE THE FIRST HALF OF Leviticus. We read about their investiture, the details of their Divine service, their role in different situations of ritual purification and, finally, the Kohen Gadol's awe-inspiring Temple service on Yom Kippur. There is, however, one exception to the flow of laws related to Kohanim in the first half of Leviticus. The last forty-six verses of *Parashas Shemini* enumerate the kosher animals. Why does the Torah insert these laws among the laws of the Kohanim? What do they have in common?

The answer may lie in the Talmudic adage (*Chagigah* 27a) that likens a person's table to an altar. In other words, just as a person offers up meat and grain on the Temple altar in order to elevate himself and draw closer to God, so should he direct his table to a similar purpose. Food should not be eaten for purely self-indulgent, gluttonous pleasure.[1] It should, rather, fortify a person in his quest for closeness to God. Accordingly, our Sages encourage us (*Avos* 3:4) to enrich our meals with Torah discussions.

Furthermore, the *Nefesh HaChaim* states that the physical structure of the *Mishkan* and later Temples mirrors human anatomy.[2] A person should see himself not as a higher form of animal but as a living temple dedicated to God, and he should consider

---

1. The Ramban understands the admonition to be holy (*Leviticus* 19:2) as a specific prohibition against gluttony.

2. My friend, Rabbi David Forman, has elaborated on this parallel. The *Aron*, which contained the Torah and was placed in the Inner Sanctum, represents the mind. To the southeast was the *Menorah* and to the southwest the *Shulchan* (Table) with the *lechem hapanim* (showbread). These represent the eyes (light) and the material world they see, as represented by the *lechem hapanim*. Further east was the Golden Altar, whose fragrance is suggestive of the nose's function. Outside the *Mishkan* and further east was the Sacrificial Altar with its long horizontal ramp, suggestive of the mouth. I would add the *Paroches*, the curtain between the Inner Sanctum and the Sanctuary, as analogous to the tentorium, an impenetrable sheath separating the brain in the upper skull from the rest of the body.

the food he eats as sacrifices offered up on the altar. God told the Jewish people (*Exodus* 25:8), "Make Me a *Mishkan* and I will dwell among them." By making a *Mishkan* for God, they themselves will become like temples, and He will dwell "among them."

Now we can understand why the Torah inserts the laws of kosher animals into the laws of the Temple service and the Kohanim. The message is clear. A person is a *Mikdash me'at*, a miniature Temple, and he must eat only those foods worthy of being brought into his sanctified body.

פרשת תזריע
Parashas Tazria

Twenty-Five Beholds

TWENTY-FIVE TIMES IN A SINGLE *PARASHAH* IS A REMARKable number of recurrences of a seemingly superfluous word. Yet this is exactly how often we encounter here the simple word *hinei* (הִנֵּה), behold. The Malbim writes that the Torah uses *hinei* to introduce something new; it suggests an element of surprise. Are there really so many surprising developments in this *parashah*? Let us take a closer look.

When a Kohen reexamines a *tzaraas* lesion on the skin, clothing or house, what would surprise him? The spread of the lesion appears to be surprising (13:36), "If the Kohen sees it, and behold (*hinei*), the affliction has spread." But then the maintenance of the status quo seems to be surprising as well (13:32), "If the Kohen sees . . . and behold (*hinei*), the affliction has not spread." Why does the Torah use the word *hinei* in both cases? How can change and no change both be surprising?

Furthermore, how do we explain the inordinate number of times the word *hinei* appears in this *parashah*? Is there perhaps a deeper connection between the number 25 and the blight of *tzaraas*?

We find points of association between the number 25 and the Kohanim, the priestly caste. For instance, the priestly blessing of the people begins with the words *ko s'varchu* (so shall you bless), and the numerical value of the word *ko* (כֹּה) is 25. Furthermore, the Torah specifies 24 different gifts, such as portions of sacrificial meat, agricultural offerings and tithes, to which the Kohanim are entitled. The Torah also grants them the privilege of blessing the Jewish nation, bringing the total to 25.[1] Finally, the festival of Chanukah celebrates the victory of the Jewish people, led by the Kohanim, against the Greek oppressors and the re-establishment of the Temple service. The word Chanukah itself, according to our Sages, is an acrostic of *chanu chaf hei* (חָנוּ כ״ה), they rested on the 25th day. Again, the number 25 occurs suggestively in relation to the Kohanim.

Let us now take a closer look at the number 25 itself. The square root of 25 is 5, a number associated with Divinity in numerous ways, such as the 5 levels of creation, the 5 levels of the soul, the 5 Books of the Torah and even the Ten Commandments that appear on two Tablets of 5 each. We further find that the Torah associates the number 5 with the very act of creation in the word *behibar'am* (בְּהִבָּרְאָם), in their creation, which is spelled in the Torah with a small *hei*. According to the Midrash, the disproportionate size of the *hei* suggests that God created the world with the letter *hei*, whose numerical value is 5.

The Maharal explains that concepts associated with a number are retained or expanded when multiplied by that number or by a factor of 10, a number in itself laden with mystical overtones. When the number is squared, he goes on to explain, it is an expansion of the idea within its particular framework. When it is multiplied by 10, however, the implications are more universal. Relating the number 25, or 5^2, back to the Kohanim with whom it is associated, we see here an affirmation of their special role as agents of God.[2]

1. Rabbi Moshe Shapiro *shlita* identified this to me as the 25th gift to the Kohanim.
2. Even the name Kohen (כֹּהֵן; *chaf, hei, nun*) may reflect this with the last *nun* whose numerical value is 50, a tenfold increase of 5.

In this light, we gain new insight into the word *hinei*. More than an indication of the unexpected or surprising, it reflects God's hidden presence at work in a way that could not have been predicted. For example, Joseph's brothers threw him into the pit, they raised their eyes (*Genesis* 27:25), "And behold (*hinei*), a caravan of Ishmaelites was passing." Here, as throughout the Torah, *hinei* conveys the notion that God's hidden providence guides the events as they enfold. The arrival of the Ishmaelite caravan heading toward Egypt just after Joseph's brothers cast him into the pit was not extraordinary or even necessarily surprising. Nonetheless, the coincidence of its arrival could not have been predicted.

Tzaraas is also a purely providential event outside the normal course of nature. The lesion results from intimate Divine intervention (*hashgachah pratis*), regardless of whether it expands, contracts or remains unchanged. It is always *hinei*.

Delving more deeply into the elegant palindrome of the word *hinei* (הִנֵּה), we find a subtle corroboration of the profound connection between these letters and Divinity. Its two distinct letters are *hei* ה and *nun* נ, whose numerical values are 5 and 50 respectively. According to the Maharal's guideline, the number 50 (5 times 10) represents a universal expansion of the idea of 5. Thus, we find the 50 levels of purity (*taharah*) and the 50 levels of impurity (*tumah*), 50 years of the *Yovel* (Jubilee year), 50 golden clasps that connect the Tabernacle, and the mysterious presence of the reverse *nun* in *Parashas Beha'aloscha*.

The Maharal further points out another aspect of their uniqueness. The *hei* and *nun* have no complementary letters with which to complete a numerical value of 10 or 100. For instance, the *aleph* and the *tes*, whose numerical values are 1 and 9 respectively, add up to 10, just as the *yud* (10) and the *tzaddi* (90) add up to 100. The *hei* (5), however, combines only with itself to add up to 10, and the *nun* (50) with itself to add up to 100.

Another aspect of the word *hinei* is that its numerical value is 60 — two times *hei* (5) equals 10, plus *nun* (50) equals 60 — the numerical value of the letter *samech* (ס). The form of the letter *samech* alludes to the concept that God, so to speak, surrounds or envelops the totality of the created universe. Its circular shape also implies that the created universe cannot create anything new ex nihilo; true creativity is the exclusive providence of God. The word *samech* itself means support, which reinforces the concept that the whole of creation depends on God's continuous will. Additionally, the number 60 is 10 times the 6 days of creation or the 6 coordinates of space (up, down and the four cardinal points of the compass).

All in all, the word *hinei*, in its letters and numerical value, confirms the concept of the natural world infused with the hidden Divine providence. And when the Torah uses this word 25 times concerning *tzaraas*, it connects this providentially formed malady with the Kohanim, who are God's agents.

In *Parashas Vayeitzei,* the word *hinei* is also emphatically present. From Jacob's initial encounter with God at Bethel when he leaves his home until he returns many years later, *hinei* occurs 10 times, and 13 times in the *parashah* overall.

The trials and tribulations of Jacob's extended separation from his home serve as the template of all future exiles; we recall his experiences when we tell the story of our exile and redemption Passover night. The appearance of *hinei* 10 times underscores God's providential presence in Jacob's thirty-six-year ordeal of separation from his parents and his homeland.[3] Among all the patriarchs, it was Jacob who established the evening prayer; night in its enveloping blackness suggests a time of surrender and trust (*emunah*). The presence of *hinei* as Jacob set out from his home reinforces the truth that God's providence guided his life in exile — just as it guides ours today.

3. The 13 expressions of *hinei* in the *parashah* in total correspond to Jacob's 13 children and the 13 tribes who would descend from him.

The Torah instructs (13:2) that the *metzora* be brought "to Aaron the Kohen or to one of his sons the Kohanim." Since there is no special requirement for the participation of the Kohen Gadol, why does the Torah single out Aaron for special mention? When the services of Kohanim are required elsewhere, such as the examination of the *sotah*, the suspected adulteress, there is no mention at all of the Kohen Gadol. Furthermore, the subsequent phrase "or to one of his sons the Kohanim" seems excessively wordy. It would have sufficed to say "or his sons."

As disciples of a great leader and teacher, the Kohanim are called upon to serve as representatives of the Kohen Gadol. This added dimension to their roles made it incumbent upon them to emulate him to the best of their abilities. This dimension emerges specifically in their management of the *tzaraas* process.

The primary cause of *tzaraas* is the sin of *lashon hara*, slanderous speech, as well as other aggressive acts. The Kohen Gadol had a special mission to deal with the sin of *lashon hara*; in one of the central services of Yom Kippur, he brought incense into the Holy of Holies to expiate the sin of *lashon hara*.

Technically speaking, the Kohen's duty with regard to *tzaraas* is to determine whether the lesions are ritually pure (*tahor*) or impure (*tamei*). But God also designated Kohanim as the teachers and mentors of the Jewish people. In this role, they must also address the moral failing that caused the *tzaraas*. To do so, thcy must draw on the example of Aaron, the first Kohen Gadol, who overflowed with love and kindness. As the Torah alludes, they must identify with the Kohen Gadol who entered the Holy of Holies on Yom Kippur to expiate the sin of *lashon hara*.

פרשת מצורע

Parashas Metzora

Intolerable Reluctance

IT MUST HAVE BEEN QUITE UNPLEASANT TO BE A *METZORA*, afflicted with *tzaraas*.[1] The unsightly lesions and the Torah-mandated quarantine made it difficult to endure. One might expect a *metzora* to initiate the purification process as quickly as possible so that he could return to normal.

But what if he took a cavalier attitude and was in no hurry to go to the Kohen to become purified? We find a clue in the language of the Torah (14:2), "This shall be the law of the *metzora* on the day of his purification — he shall be brought to the Kohen." Instead of using the active "he shall go to the Kohen," the Torah uses the passive "he shall be brought to the Kohen." This implies that he may be brought to the Kohen by force.

Since the Torah finds it necessary to specify that we may force a *metzora* to comply with the laws that pertain to him, it would appear that this is not the case with regard to other command-

1. *Tzaraas* is often mistranslated as leprosy. It is really a nonclinical affliction that discolors the body, clothing or residence and results in ritual impurity (*tumah*).

ments. In fact, however, the possibility of enforced compliance exists with regard to just about all the commandments. In what way does the case of a *metzora* stand out?

The commandments of the Torah fall into two categories: positive commandments (*mitzvos asei*) and prohibitions (*mitzvos lo saaseh*). According to the *Shulchan Aruch* (*Choshen Mishpat* 4), we may use nonlethal force to prevent the transgression of a prohibition, and lethal force only in extreme cases, such as to prevent a murder. Lethal force may also be used to coerce a neglectful person to fulfill a positive commandment; as the Talmud (*Kesubos* 86a) states, "He is beaten to within an inch of his life."

The laws of *metzora* fall into the category of positive commandments. What additional guidelines regarding the use of force apply to them, as suggested by the verse?

There is a disagreement on this issue in the *Shulchan Aruch*. In general, according to *Ketzos HaChoshen,* only rabbinical judges and not laypeople may use potentially lethal force to gain compliance with positive commandments. But with regard to *tzaraas*, any individual may exert life-threatening force to bring the *metzora* to the Kohen.

Nesivos HaMishpat disagrees; he maintains that the use of lethal force is never restricted to rabbinical judges. Laypeople have the right to force compliance of any positive commandments on their recalcitrant brothers. With *tzaraas*, however, they have not only a right but also an obligation.

According to both views, the Torah broadens the scope of the license to use lethal force to effect compliance with the laws of *tzaraas*. Why?

Let us first consider the difference between positive commandments and prohibitions. Penalties for the violation of prohibitions are generally more severe; they often entail capital punishment, corporal punishment or untimely death. The penalties for violation of positive commandments are almost never so severe. Yet paradoxically, the Torah permits lethal force to assure compliance with a positive commandment but not with a prohibition. How do we explain this?

The answer lies in a basic distinction between positive commandments and prohibitions. A person who contemplates the transgression of a prohibition has not yet done anything wrong; although he is considering rebellion, he has not actually taken the step. Therefore, we may not apply lethal force to restrain him, even though the potential sin is grave.

On the other hand, when a person rejects a positive commandment that comes his way, he is instantly in violation. He rebels against God every moment he refuses to act. This person has violated his very *raison d'être*, and there is no limit to the force we may exert to curtail his rebellion.

Now let us consider why the Torah indicates an added requirement and urgency to curtail the rebellion of a *metzora* who fails to comply with the laws of *tzaraas*.

Our Sages deduce the cause of *tzaraas* from the two instances of its occurrence in the Torah. In the first (*Exodus* 4:6-8), Moses doubts that the people will believe he is God's messenger, and God afflicts his arm with *tzaraas* as a sign of his mission. Later on (*Numbers* 12:10), Moses' sister Miriam was critical of him for separating from his wife after reaching his level of prophecy; Miriam is stricken with *tzaraas*. Moses and Miriam spoke improperly, and the Sages deduce that *tzaraas* is caused primarily by the sin of *lashon hara*.

Let us reflect. Most sins have no immediate physical manifestations. Why then did God create *tzaraas* as a sign of the sin of *lashon hara*?

The Talmud considers misfortune a warning signal of wrongdoing and a call for self-examination, but there is no absolute surety. Misfortune is not always a sign of overt providence; it may come independent of sin (*yissurim shel ahavah*), and in any case, it appears to occur through natural means. *Tzaraas*, however, is an exception; it is always an external supernatural manifestation of an internal failing. If there is *tzaraas*, there is sin. *Tzaraas* is the only halachic institution that serves as a type of interface between the legal system and an expression of God's supernatural providential hand; God intervenes in the laws of nature to create the malady.

In this light, we can understand why failure to comply with the laws of *tzaraas* is a far greater rebellion than failure to comply with other positive commandments. Once God shows the afflicted providentially and publicly that he has sinned, he must go to the Kohen to expiate his sin. His rejection of this obligation is a flagrant affront to God, and it is incumbent on all of Israel to set him right.

Although *tzaraas* is the result of sin, the only two people mentioned in the Torah who actually contracted this malady are Moses and Miriam, two of the most perfectly righteous people that ever appeared on the face of the earth. There is no happenstance in the Torah; the choice of these two as the paradigm of *tzaraas* sufferers is surely instructive.

By any objective measure, these two stellar personalities were righteous beyond our conception. Nonetheless, relative to their own potential, there must have been some minuscule failing that manifested itself through the *tzaraas*. The Torah's message is that it is not for us to pass judgment when we encounter someone afflicted with *tzaraas*, or any suffering for that matter, since it reflects a failing relative to his potential. In the case of Moses or Miriam, it may be a failing we cannot even begin to fathom.

פרשת אחרי מות
Parashas Acharei Mos

i. *The Oscillating Universe*

ALL YEAR LONG, THE KOHEN GADOL WORE A SET OF EIGHT garments embroidered with gold and studded with jewels; they were called "the golden vestments." When he entered the Holy of Holies on Yom Kippur, however, he wore four simple garments called "the white vestments."

The Kohen Gadol performed his elaborate Yom Kippur service in five stages, alternating between golden and white vestments. Each time he donned a set of vestments he immersed in a *mikveh*, a total of five times. In addition to the five full immersions, the Kohen Gadol washed his hands and feet ten times during the day's service, twice for each vestment change.

There is a dispute between the Rabbis and Rabbi Meir in the Talmud (*Yoma* 34b) concerning the two washings per vestment change. Both agree that the second washing took place after he donned the new vestments. But when did the first washing take place? Rabbi Meir maintains it was just prior to donning the vestments. The Rabbis maintain he washed his hands prior to removing the previous vestments and immersing in the *mikveh*.

At first glance, Rabbi Meir's view seems more logical. First, the Kohen Gadol washes his hands and feet to sanctify himself for the act of donning a new set of holy vestments. Once he dons the vestments, he washes his hands and feet again to sanctify himself for the Divine service he is about to perform. But what purpose can we assign to washing his hands and feet prior to removing the previous vestments, as the Rabbis contend? Why does the act of removing holy vestments require a special sanctification?

Kabbalistic literature discusses a profound concept known as *ratzo vashav*, being desired and withdrawing, which describes the course of a human being's advance toward perfection. Man's nature imposes limitations on his ascent toward clinging to God (*d'veikus*), and he often needs to pause to catch his breath, so to speak, before he goes farther. We find this dynamic in the psychological realm as well, where dreams integrate and process the avalanche of emotionally charged information we accumulate every day; without the respite of dreams we would suffer overload.

The phenomena of the Sabbath (seven days) and the fallow years of the *Shemittah* (seven years) and *Yovel* (seven seven-year cycles) can be thought of as a sort of oscillation between activity and passivity, as a withdrawal from productive activity that allows us to achieve a higher spiritual elevation.

On a national level, we see this stop-and-go dynamic in the Jewish people's experience in the desert, where the splitting of the sea and the revelation at Sinai were followed by interludes of recidivism. They erected a *Mishkan* for the Divine Presence only to succumb shortly afterwards to the cajolery of the spies.

The Jewish people traversed forty-nine separate and unique journeys in the desert. The fiftieth — with significant symbolic

1. Rashi (*Deuteronomy* 10:6) enumerates eight stops in reverse, which translates to seven journeys.

overtones — was the entry to the Holy Land. Seven of these were regressions in the opposite direction.[1] Thus, one in seven journeys was one of withdrawal, similar to the punctuation of the seven-day week and the seven-year *Shemittah* by one unit of respite.

Although in these instances the backsliding involved sin, this is not a necessary component of the *shav* phase.

Perhaps the tendency for oscillation may mirror creation itself, which is, according to Kabbalistic literature, a fine-tuned balance between the expansive force of God's act of kindness (*chessed*) and the limiting force of His strict justice (*din*), as reflected in the Divine Name of *Shad-dai*.

The Rabbis' view of the ten washings of Yom Kippur may reflect this need for a withdrawal phase in the consolidation of religious experience. They ruled that a Kohen Gadol must wash his hands and feet before removing a set of holy vestments. He too must sanctify and consecrate his act of removal and withdrawal. By it, too, he comes closer to God.

ii. *The Guilty Speaker*

WHICH OF THE ACTS PERFORMED BY THE KOHEN GADOL ON Yom Kippur was most central to the day? Was it the special sacrificial service of the day, the communal animal offerings whose blood was sprinkled within the Holy of Holies? Was it the dramatic sending of the goat to Azazel where it was pushed to its death off a jagged cliff? Or was it something else?

A careful scrutiny of the structure of the Yom Kippur service suggests it was the burning of aromatic incense (*ketores*) on a pan of embers within the Holy of Holies. The special Yom Kippur service of the Kohen Gadol began when he donned the "white vestments." After preparing and slaughtering the bull, he brought the *ketores* into the Holy of Holies and poured it onto the burning coals. He then proceeded to perform all the special activities of the day, changing vestments twice in the process. When he finished, he returned to the Holy of Holies to remove the pan in which the fire had consumed the *ketores*. In essence, the presence of the burning *ketores* in the Holy of Holies preceded and qualified everything else the Kohen Gadol did that was unique to Yom Kippur; any activities performed out of sequence with relation to the *ketores* were disallowed.

What was the purpose of the special Yom Kippur *ketores*? For what did it atone? The Talmud (*Yoma* 44a) explains that it atoned for *lashon hara*, malicious speech; "let [the burning of the incense], which is done in private [in the Holy of Holies], atone for sins committed in private [specifically *lashon hara*, which is usually spoken behind the victim's back]."

Isn't it astounding that on the holiest day of the year, in the holiest place on earth, the man holding the holiest office in the world focuses primarily on the sin of malicious speech? Not murder, not theft, not libidinous impropriety, not sins against God, but malicious speech! How are we to understand the centrality of this sin, which is after all only one of words?

On the sixth day of creation (*Genesis* 2:7), "God formed man from the dust of the ground, and He breathed the soul of life into his nostrils, and man became a living being." Onkelos translates the words "living being" as *ruach memalela*, a spirit that speaks. The essence of a human being is reflected in his ability to communicate thoughts through speech.

Lashon hara subverts this life-defining speech in order to vent jealousy, hatred and otherwise aggressive feelings toward others. Underlying his act, the speaker of *lashon hara* wants to destroy his victim. Psychoanalytic theory holds that verbal aggressiveness is a remnant of a child's personality called magical thinking; children tend to think their thoughts and words have power. Adults continue to employ this mechanism of the mind. But in the absence of physical violence, the aggressor deludes himself that he has done nothing wrong when he has in fact acted out through words his wish to cause damage or even annihilation.

What motivates the speaker of *lashon hara* to act so aggressively? Our Sages give us the answer by equating *lashon hara* with idolatry. Idolatry stems from man's egotism, which allows him to fashion and control his own gods. Speaking *lashon hara* also stems from the speaker's assumption that the world revolves around him. Feeling threatened by the success of others, success he feels should be coming to him, the speaker uses speech to commit aggression stealthily and without accountability. As such, *lashon hara* reflects profound corruption and is central in the service of the Kohen Gadol on Yom Kippur. Our Sages underscore this point by observing that every person is guilty of at least *avak lashon hara*, slight traces of slanderous speech.

While the *ketores* offering served to atone for the nation's sins at some level, the value of that atonement was greatest for each individual who understood that the Kohen Gadol's activities were a model for his own. Just as the Kohen Gadol entered the Inner Sanctum to achieve atonement for *lashon hara* with the *ketores*, so must the guilty speaker probe the inner recesses of his heart and soul in order to effect a meaningful penitence. Just as the Kohen Gadol was alone as he performed his service, so must the guilty speaker find the courage to take the painful journey of self-scrutiny on his own and make meaningful changes in his personality.

iii. Over and Under

WHAT ARE WE SUPPOSED TO DO WITH THE BLOOD OF slaughtered birds and animals of the wild? The Torah commands (17:13) that we take some soil and cover it — *be'afar*. The Talmud (*Chullin* 31a, 83b; *Beitzah* 7b) records a dispute among the Sages as to the exact method of covering the blood. The dispute hinges on the translation of the word *be'afar*. Rabbi Zeira translates it as "in soil" and requires that we place soil both below and above the blood, encapsulating it "in" soil. The Rabbis, however, translate the word as "with soil," and therefore, they consider it sufficient to allow the blood to spill onto the ground and have one place soil only above it.

Is this a purely grammatical dispute or is there also a conceptual disagreement? Many disputes in the Talmud that seem to involve grammatical hairsplitting reveal profound underlying distinctions upon closer scrutiny. Is that the case here as well?

Furthermore, how are we to understand Rabbi Zeira's ruling? What difference does it make if soil is placed underneath the blood since it is falling on the ground in any case?

All commandments are without question beneficial to those who perform them, but that benefit may be realized in two different ways. One, the very act itself may be directly beneficial to the one who performs it. Two, the act may accomplish good in the world at large, which indirectly benefits the one who is responsible for bringing that good to the world. Often, of course, both features are present. Giving charity, for instance, is an act that builds character and spiritual stature while providing much needed food and shelter for the poor recipients.

This distinction may be seen in a famous rabbinic dispute concerning the obligation to send away the mother bird before taking the eggs in her nest (*shiluach haken*). In the Rambam's view, this commandment expresses the Torah's compassion for the mother bird, sparing her the sorrow of seeing her young snatched away before her eyes. Accordingly, the direct benefit of the commandment is to the bird, and the indirect benefit is to the one who sends her away and thereby acts virtuously. The Ramban argues that we find no such compassion expressed toward other creatures. Rather, the commandment seeks to inculcate compassion in the one who sends away the mother bird; he is the direct beneficiary.

We may discern this same distinction in the dispute between Rabbi Zeira and the Rabbis regarding the covering of the blood. Apparently, the Torah wanted a covering of the blood. Why is this so? Is it because the state of blood being covered is somehow spiritually desirable in and of itself? Or is the act of covering it the desired goal?

According to the Rabbis, the Torah desires the end result of having the blood covered. Man's participation in the commandment is to effect this end result; its benefit to him is indirect. Therefore, as long as he participates by sprinkling soil from above while the ground sheathes the blood from below, the desired goal is achieved; he has fulfilled his obligation.

According to Rabbi Zeira, however, the very act of covering is the commandment's objective. Man benefits directly by the very nature of his act. Placing soil only above the blood is insufficient. Although for all practical purposes the blood is covered both over and under, the act of covering is nonetheless incomplete. Therefore, Rabbi Zeira requires that we place soil both above and under the freshly spilled blood.

פרשת קדושים
Parashas Kedoshim

i. The Royal Road to Holiness

HOLINESS ENTAILS GOING BEYOND THE LETTER OF THE LAW to come closer to God. "You shall be holy," the Torah instructs (19:2), "for I, God, your Lord, am holy." As the Ramban explains, emulating God's ways is the means by which to achieve the ultimate goal of human perfection. The observance of the commandments is the starting point, the absolute basis from which we catapult ourselves toward the higher goal of clinging to Him (*d'veikus*).

Let us take a look at the commandments that immediately follow this powerful admonition to seek holiness (19:3-4). "Every man: your mother and father shall you revere, My Sabbath shall you observe, I am God, your Lord. Do not turn to idols nor shall you make for yourselves molten gods. I am God, your Lord."

We can easily understand why idolatry is so inimical to the holiness achieved by clinging to God. But why are honoring parents and observing the Sabbath the first commandments on the road to holiness? How do they help us reach this exalted but elusive goal?

According to our Sages, God gave these two commandments to the Jewish people in Marah shortly after they left Egypt, even before they arrived at Mount Sinai. This is borne out by the language of the Ten Commandments (*Deuteronomy* 5:15-16), which adds the expression "as I commanded you" to the commandments of keeping the Sabbath and honoring parents. Our Sages, by oral tradition, identify these as the laws God gave at Marah a month earlier (*Exodus* 15:25). Why were these two commandments singled out? The Maharal explains that Sabbath observance recalls creation and the Exodus and acknowledges God's general providence (*hashgachah klalis*). And honoring parents, the conduits through which God introduces all souls into the world, is a clear acknowledgment of God's specific providence *(hashgachah pratis*).

These two commandments appear among the first five of the Ten Commandments, which address man's relationship with God; they both engender an awareness of His providence and thereby facilitate our progress toward holiness. Life offers many unexpected twists, frustrations and seeming misfortunes, which at times appear disproportionate and undeserved. A person may feel dispirited, or he may ignore the message implicit in his ordeal. But a person with strong faith in Divine providence will rise above his travails. He will recognize God's guiding hand through the seemingly capricious shoals of life. He will learn from them and proceed undaunted along the royal road to holiness.

ii. The Inward Cause of Giving

HARVESTS ARE A TIME OF BOUNTY NOT ONLY FOR OURselves but for the poor people as well (19:9-10). "When you reap the harvest of your land, you shall not cut to the corner of your field, nor shall you take the [dropped] sheaves of your harvest. You shall not take the single grapes of your vineyard nor shall you gather the fallen fruit of your vineyard; leave them for the poor and the stranger; I am God, your Lord."

The Torah gives the landowner two distinct instructions about the remnants of his harvest — "you shall not take" and "leave them for the poor" — that seem redundant. If he "does not take them," he has obviously "left them," and vice versa. What are we meant to learn from the seemingly superfluous language?

The Talmud (*Yoma* 36b) cites two differing views. Rabbi Yosi HaGlili contends that initially there is only the single prohibition "not to take," but if a person inadvertently or deliberately takes the produce, the positive commandment to return it and "leave it" for the poor takes effect. Rabbi Akiva, however, sees the prohibition and the positive commandment as parallel and simultaneous; whoever leaves the produce had fulfilled both, and whoever takes it has violated both. Rabbi Akiva further maintains that if the landowner takes the produce unlawfully, he has sinned doubly but he need not return the produce to the field.

Rabbi Akiva's view seems problematic. What does the positive commandment to "leave" the produce in the field accomplish? Whenever the Torah duplicates a requirement or restriction, each command must be understood to emphasize a different aspect or value of the performance. What added element does the second commandment reveal?

Rabbi Akiva apparently discerns two aspects to the commands concerning agricultural remnants. One obvious aspect of leaving produce in the field for the poor is the expression of compassion for the needy; this is the positive commandment. According to Rabbi Akiva, there is also an independent, inward-looking benefit in the landowner's restricting his pursuit of materialism; if we recognize God's complete sovereignty, we need not chase every last grain of wheat that falls to the ground. The prohibition curbs the potential cupidity of the landowner, while the positive commandment to "leave" calls for actively supporting the poor and alleviating their hunger.

iii. Speech Bares the Soul

NUMEROUS PROHIBITIONS THROUGHOUT THE TORAH address the sin of *lashon hara* (slanderous speech). One of the most famous appears in *Parashas Kedoshim* (19:16), "Do not walk about bearing tales among your people."

God created man and made him into a "living being," which *Targum Onkelos* translates (*Genesis* 2:7) as a *ruach memalela*, a spirit that speaks. Speech is the interface between the physical and the intellectual. Man's ability to speak defines him. From a psychological perspective, speech can reveal the deepest, most carefully concealed attitudes of the speaker. Often, a person vents and gives satisfaction to his inner feelings through words. When a person speaks *lashon hara*, his malicious words allow him to gain a feeling of superiority. All the while, he tells himself he has committed no aggressive acts, that he is not a mean-spirited person. But this is self-delusion. Our Sages say that "the tongue holds the power of life and death"; *lashon hara* can destroy lives and often does. Ironically, perhaps no one suffers more than the frequent slanderer himself, who becomes steeped in his most primitive drives.

At the same time, there is a great opportunity in the internal battle against *lashon hara*. It brings a person face to face with his underlying pettiness or baser desires as he restrains his inclination to speak. A person who resists the *lashon hara* impulse delivers a powerful impetus to his own spiritual growth and development.

Because of their deep understanding of the dangers of *lashon hara* and the benefits of the struggle against it, our Sages shunned idle conversation and any type of utterance that may stem from underlying aggressiveness or other base instincts.

The Talmud (*Pesachim* 3b) discusses the lengths to which we must go in order to avoid bad speech. For instance, our Sages counseled against being a bearer of bad news.[1] Several base emotions are satisfied by bearing bad tidings. Informing others about a death, for example, may give the speaker, at some level, a sense of control over death. He may also unconsciously be satisfying aggressive feelings toward the one who will be bereaved.

The Talmud tells an anecdote (ibid.) about Yochanan Chakukah, who had just arrived from the country. The Rabbis asked him if the wheat crop had been good. Careful to avoid being the direct bearer of bad news, Yochanan responded indirectly that the barley crop had been good. The Rabbis did not find this response about barley, which is used primarily for animal feed, subtle enough. "Go tell the horses and donkeys," they said sarcastically. What should he have said? The Talmud offers two suggestions. He could have said, "Last year's crop was good." Or else, "The lentil crop [usually eaten by humans] was good." These preferred responses not only avoided conveying bad news directly, they were also associated with something pleasant. This subtle but significant improvement reflects the Sages' understanding that speech is a window to the soul. Man gains tremendous advantage in the micromanagement of his speech.

Let us take a further look at the verse prohibiting *lashon hara* (19:16), "Do not walk about bearing tales among your people; do not stand upon the blood of your neighbor; I am God."

What is the meaning of "standing on the blood of your neighbor"? Our Sages (*Sanhedrin* 73a; *Toras Kohanim*) derive from this

---

1. It is appropriate that this discussion occurs in *Pesachim*, one of whose etymological derivations is *peh sach*, the mouth speaks, a homiletic reference to the retelling of the story of the Exodus on Passover.

statement the obligation to rescue an endangered person and the prohibition against suppressing evidence in a court case. Both these laws, which prohibit causing harm through inaction, subtly connect to the first half of the verse. Yet the verse invites a further connection by its contrasting metaphors of "walking" and "standing."

Perhaps this language is also the source of our Sages' admonition that the crime of listening to slander is worse than the crime of speaking it. One of the more insidious features of *lashon hara* is that the speaker easily avoids facing up to the destructiveness of his aggressive act; he tells himself he bears no responsibility, that it was only words. Yet at some level, he knows he is acting out his aggressive feelings, albeit in a lesser way; he is a "walker." The one who listens to slander, however, has done nothing premeditated or deliberate. He usually has only a moment's notice before the slander starts to flow, and it is exceedingly easy for him to shrug off all responsibility for what was no more than passive acquiescence; he sees himself as a blameless "bystander." Therefore, the Torah specifically admonishes him in the starkest terms, "Do not stand on the blood of your neighbor, I am God." Listening to slander is the emotional equivalent of passive acquiescence to murder.

iv. *Reproof, the Second Time Around*

MUCH OF DEUTERONOMY FEATURES MOSES' REPROOFS TO the Jewish nation on the last day of his life. The *Sifrei* offers four reasons for postponing rebuke until the time of death. One of these is to avoid repeated rebukes.

What is the problem with having to rebuke someone twice?

The *Sifrei* gives no reason. The Torah, in fact, places no limit on the number of times one should rebuke someone who violates its commandments (19:17), "You shall not hate your brother in your heart; you shall surely reprove your friend and not bear a sin because of him." Apparently, the avoidance of repeated rebukes is a practical rather than a legal consideration.

One danger of repeated rebukes is that they seem to express annoyance with the one rebuked for ignoring the first reprimand. The one receiving criticism may sense that the second reproach flows from the rebuker's anger rather than concern. He may perceive the rebuke as an expression of the reprimander's superiority, which gives him the right to criticize. How can such rebuke be effective? To accept it would be a tacit acknowledgment of the rebuker's superiority. The rebuked is more likely to reject it; even if he accepts it, he will be resentful. A deathbed rebuke, however, avoids this problem and is easily accepted as sincere.

Accordingly, we see the verse in a new light. "Do not hate your brother in your heart." In other words, remove all hate from your heart before you offer criticism to someone else. Otherwise, it will not be fully accepted. But if the rebuke stems from a love of one's fellow man and a desire to see the implementation of God's will, then in a relative sense the rebuker never rebukes more than once. There is never a sense that the rebuker is criticizing a second time because his first rebuke was ignored. Even after a hundred rebukes, the rebuker is not personally disturbed when he is not fully effective and feels no sense of personal annoyance that he has done it ninety-nine times before. His persistence is altruistic and benign, and the rebuked does not feel antagonized.

vi. The Essence of Holiness

APPARENTLY, THE TORAH WAS NOT SATISFIED WITH JUST two mentions of the prohibition against *ov* and *yid'oni*, consulting diviners of the future. After enumerating the laws governing a holy lifestyle, the Torah returns for a third time to the same prohibition at the *parashah's* conclusion (20:26-27). Why is this prohibition so central to the theme of achieving holiness, the overriding theme of this *parashah*?

Perhaps the frequent refrain of "I am God" in this *parashah* gives us a clue. People are not naturally endowed with extrasensory perception such that they can know the future. Its absence facilitates moral free will and trust in Divine providence. Consulting a sorcerer thwarts our opportunity to trust in God's providence and to allow reason, based on the Torah, to guide our decisions and choices. If the ultimate goal of living in holiness is to bring us closer to God, then the practice of *ov* and *yid'oni* is the antithesis of holiness, and the extreme emphasis on the prohibition is fully understood.

Each of the three prohibitions against *ov* and *yid'oni* is expressed differently. First, the Torah commands us (19:31) not to "turn to [them]," then (20:6), not to "lust after them," and finally (20:27), "if there be among you an *ov* or *yid'oni* . . ."

A progressive pattern emerges. The contact with the *ov* and *yid'oni* begins with a curious interest, with "turning to them." But soon, it develops into a much stronger interest, a "lust after them." And finally, it takes over completely, so that the once curious is himself now a full-fledged *ov* and *yid'oni* "among you," the Jewish people. As the Talmud (*Shabbos* 104b) warns, if the evil inclination is not held in check it chips away in small incremental steps until it attains full dominion.

פרשת אמור
Parashas Emor

i. Holiness Is Not Elitism

KOHANIM ARE NOT JUST BENEFICIARIES OF SPECIAL PRIVIleges. They also have special restrictions (21:1). "And God said to Moses, 'Speak to the Kohanim, the sons of Aaron, and tell them: Each of you shall not contaminate himself to a [dead] person among his people.' "

A puzzling question arises when we examine the sequence of the *parshios* in Leviticus. The first six *parshios* address the Divine service, the investiture of the Kohanim, their priestly duties and responsibilities and the Yom Kippur service. The seventh, *Parashas Kedoshim*, discusses general rules that apply to laymen and Kohanim equally, giving the impression that the subject of Kohanim had been exhausted. But then, the Torah returns to the Kohanim right here in *Parashas Emor*. Why does the Torah digress from the subject of Kohanim only to return to it once again one *parashah* later?

The Kovner Rav takes notes of the aforementioned phrase "speak to the Kohanim, the sons of Aaron." What is the purpose, he wonders, of the seemingly redundant words "the sons of Aaron"?

They carry an important message to the Kohanim, he explains. Having been instructed so intensively on the exclusivity of their role in Jewish life, they might consider themselves an elite group superior to other Jews, especially in view of the Kohanim's stringent requirements for ritual purity outlined here. The Torah, therefore, reminds them that they are descended from Aaron, a man of humility and boundless love for every individual Jew, a man who looked down at no one.

Perhaps the placement of the prohibitions against priestly contamination in *Parashas Emor* can also be explained by the specter of elitism, but from the other side. Just as the Torah did not want the Kohanim to consider themselves an elite, it did not want the rest of the people to consider themselves second-class Jews.

Had the Torah immediately presented the restrictions imposed on the priestly caste, people might have attributed to them an innate superiority, such that the Kohanim required additional protection from contamination. Instead, the Torah presents *Parashas Kedoshim*, which begins with an exhortation to every Jew to be holy and live a holy life. "For I am God, your Lord," the Torah repeats time and again, teaching us to sanctify every aspect of our lives by emulating God's ways. Once the Jewish people absorbed and understood the concept of holiness and withdrawal from the mundane, they would see clearly that the Kohanim required special restriction not because of innate superiority but because of the nature of their priestly duties.

Another solution to the redundancy of "the Kohanim, the sons of Aaron," as noted by the Kovner Rav, may be derived from the Talmud's description (*Taanis* 15b) of the supplementary prayer service during a drought. The *chazzan* signals the Kohanim in the synagogue to sound the *shofar*, alternating between *tekiah* sounds (long and flat) and *teruah* sounds (a series of quivering staccato blasts). The *chazzan* calls out, "*Tekiah*, Kohanim, *tekiah!*" And they sound a *tekiah*. Then the *chazzan* calls out, "*Teruah*, sons of Aaron, *teruah*!" And they sound a *teruah*.

Why are the Kohanim addressed differently in the alternating signals to sound the *shofar*? How do the *tekiah* and *teruah* relate to the respective titles "Kohanim" and "sons of Aaron"?

In a metaphysical sense, the Kohanim occupy the middle space between heaven and earth. On one hand, they are God's emissaries to instruct, implement and supervise the ritual life of the people; this aspect of their service is reflected in the title Kohanim. They also represent the people as their teachers, as well as through the sacrificial service they perform on their behalf; this special role, an outgrowth of Aaron's overflowing love for his fellow man, is reflected in the title "sons of Aaron."

The long and straight *tekiah* blast heralds man's attention toward God, and it is appropriate that those bearing the title Kohanim should sound it. The staccato *teruah* sound mimics crying; it is a call to introspection and repentance, and it is appropriate that those bearing the title "sons of Aaron," as representatives of their Jewish brethren, should sound it.

When the Torah instructs the Kohanim to guard their holiness and refrain from coming into contact with anything that defiles them, they are addressed as both "Kohanim" and "sons of Aaron." The implication is that the integrity of both their roles requires a higher standard of holiness.

ii. *Small Steps to Corruption*

DURING THE SECOND TEMPLE ERA, THE OFFICE OF KOHEN Gadol unfortunately became corrupt. More often than not, the position went to the highest bidder, usually irreligious people who denied the authority of the very Oral Law God had delegated them to teach and uphold. The Talmud (*Yoma* 18a) records that over three hundred men served as Kohen Gadol during the 420 years of the Second Temple's existence,[1] in sharp contrast to the eighteen during the 410-year existence of the First Temple.

How was it possible that this holiest of institutions became so corrupt? How did the nation permit it?

The Talmud records the first purchase of this office; Marta bas Baisus bought it for Yehoshua ben Gamla, her husband. The Tosaphists (*Bava Basra* 21a) shed a little more light on this episode by revealing that Yehoshua was a righteous person, but not the most righteous of his brethren. One of the criteria for the selection of a Kohen Gadol was that he be (21:10) "exalted above his brethren." According to the Talmud (ibid.), he was to be superior to all other Kohanim in strength, appearance, wealth and righteousness. Yehoshua fell short and still became Kohen Gadol.

Initially, the people would never have tolerated the purchase of the sacred office of Kohen Gadol by a corrupt individual; there would have been a tremendous hue and cry. But when a righteous man such as Yehoshua ben Gamla acquired the office, the people condoned what seemed like a minor infraction. After all, he was not an unworthy candidate. Later, when corrupt people began to buy the office, the shock was not so great. The people had become desensitized to the evil, and although the majority most probably disapproved, they were not outraged enough to rise up in protest. The road downhill started with a small step.

iii. Two Faces of the Convert

AS WE CELEBRATE THE BOUNTY OF THE LAND ON THE FESTIVAL of Shavuos, the Torah reminds us not to forget the poor (23:22). "When you reap the harvest of your

1. Most of these unworthy men perished upon entering the Holy of Holies on Yom Kippur.

land, you shall not cut to the corner of your field as you reap, nor shall you take the [dropped] sheaves of your harvest, leave them for the poor and the convert; I am God, your Lord."

Two forms of entitlements are described here — the corner of the field, called *pe'ah*, and the dropped sheaves, called *leket*.[2] The Torah demands that we leave these for the landless convert[3] and pauper so that they too may share in God's benevolence.

There is also a third entitlement, called *shik'chah*, the forgotten sheaves (*Deuteronomy* 25:19), "When you reap your harvest in your field, and you forget a bundle in the field, you shall not return to take it; it shall remain for the convert, orphan and widow, so that God, your Lord, will bless you in all your handiwork."

Two prominent features distinguish these two verses. One, the Torah commands us to leave the *pe'ah* and *leket* to the convert and the poor, while the *shik'chah* is to remain for converts, widows and orphans. Second, the entitlement of *pe'ah* and *leket* is expressed in the active voice, "leave it to them," while the *shik'chah* is left to them passively, "it shall remain for them."

Three questions arise. Why is *shik'chah* omitted in this *parashah*? Why are widows and orphans only included as beneficiaries of *shik'chah* as opposed to the convert who gets both? Why does the Torah express the entitlement to *shik'chah* in the passive voice, "it shall remain for them"?

During a harvest, a landowner naturally tends to round out the corners of the field as he harvests, and if he is law-abiding, he will invariably leave one corner uncut, *pe'ah*; he must also leave those stray stalks that invariably fall to the ground, *leket*. The Torah does not want him to make the extra effort to reap these inevitable harvest remnants; rather, he is to leave them for the indigent. In effect, then, by sharing in every harvest, the landless convert and the poor, who are usually also landless, become partners of sorts

2. *Leket* includes solitary items, such as a single grape on the vine; it may not be picked.
3. The convert referenced here is a *ger toshav*, a gentile who accepts upon himself the Seven Noahide Laws and thereby gains permission to reside in Israel permanently.

in his fields. This is the Torah's conceptual message here; these inevitable field remnants belong to them. But since bundled sheaves are not necessarily forgotten in every harvest, the *shik'chah* entitlement is not mentioned until Deuteronomy.

In fact, the Talmud derives that the entitlements of *pe'ah* and *leket* belong to widows and orphans as well as converts. Nonetheless, the Torah makes special mention of the convert, because he is completely without support. He is landless and has no extended family on whom to fall back in times of need.

The widow and the orphan are somewhat similar to the convert in that they, more than other poor people, are the elements of a society most easily forgotten. Thus, when Deuteronomy presents the entitlement of *shik'chah*, the sheaves forgotten in the field, it is appropriate that the Torah singles out the people who tend to be forgotten. God also shows His special concern for these forsaken groups by expressing the entitlement in the passive voice, "it shall remain for them," suggesting that it belongs to them, a gift from God. The active voice, "leave it to them," used for the corner of the field and dropped stalks, gives the impression that it is the gift of the landowner and comes from God only indirectly, through His command. Here though, what is forgotten belongs to the ones God has not forsaken.

iv. *Crying Like a Baby*

WHEREIN LIES THE SECRET OF THE MYSTERIOUS TUG OF THE *shofar* sounds? What is the significance of the long blast of the *tekiah*, the gasping *shevarim*, the tremulous *teruah* and the blast of the *tekiah* once again to bring the set to a conclusion?

Rabbinic literature discusses extensively the deeper meaning of the sounds and patterns. The Ramban, for instance, sees them as an acoustic metaphor of Divine judgment on Rosh Hashanah. The opening and closing flat *tekiah* sounds represent the outer appearance of strict justice, and the broken sounds in between allude to the mercy found within.

Perhaps we can offer additional insight into the specific nature of the sounds. The Torah states (23:24), "Speak to the people of Israel, saying, 'In the seventh month, on the first of the month, you shall have a Sabbath, trumpet calls (*teruah*) of remembrance, a holy convocation.' " According to the Talmud (*Rosh Hashanah* 33b), the middle *teruah* sound has two forms, the punctuated *shevarim* and the tremulous *teruah*, which together resemble a cry.

In considering the physiology of crying, a baby's spontaneous and artless cry offers the best model for a perfectly natural act of crying. An upsetting event takes place, such as the baby bumping its head. The baby is often immobile for a moment or two, shocked into inaction by the sudden threat to its equilibrium.

The first deep gasping cries that issue forth from the baby's mouth are not expressions of exasperation or sadness. They are actually a sharp intake of air with accompanying sound. Human physiology demands that we breathe when oxygen levels get low, and the baby instinctively recovers his breath in a few short gasps. Although the infant cannot articulate his thought, he has discovered with shock that the world can present nasty surprises. He is so shocked that he initially breathes only because his body forces him to; he utters short gasping sounds. But presently, the shock wears off, and the baby shifts into a rapid sobbing cry. Although he is unable to express himself, the rapid sounds of his crying reveal that he mourns the loss of his comfort and safety.

On Rosh Hashanah, the voice of the *shofar* is a metaphor of our own shocked then sad sounds as we face the judgment of the Heavenly Court. The first long *tekiah* blast heralds the majestic presence of God at this ceremonial acknowledgment of His Divine reign. Reflexively, as the awareness of God's nearness penetrates our consciousness, we are shocked and astonished by what we find. We have acted brazenly in a world that is not ours. We come face to face with our errors — the squandered opportunities, the debasement, the shame — and we are shocked to our very core. The gasping *shevarim* sounds reflect our shocked state; our initial shame has paralyzed our breathing, and we try to recover our breath. Only then do we give expression to our sorrow and regret by a burst of anguished wailing, symbolized by the tremulous *teruah*.

The second heraldic *tekiah* blast brings us back to the central theme of Rosh Hashanah. It is, after all, not a time to focus on personal needs and failings, for even this is a form of self-absorption. Rather, our task on Rosh Hashanah is to acknowledge and reaffirm our loyalty to God as King of the Universe. The brief flash of introspection leading to a recognition of our own unworthiness facilitates our recognition of God's awesome majesty. Now the second *tekiah* sound summons us to return to the essential task of the day — the celebration of His Divine reign.

v. Second Chances

HINDSIGHT IS ALWAYS TWENTY-TWENTY, GOES THE POPULAR saying. According to the Talmud (*Avodah Zarah* 3a), the gentile nations rejected the Torah when God offered it to them, but they will change their minds in the future. When they witness the reward of the Jewish people, they will ask for a second chance, which God will grant. He will offer them the easy, inexpensive commandment of sitting in a *succah*. At first, they will embrace it. But when it gets hot, they will abandon the *succah*, kicking at it as they leave, thereby showing themselves unworthy of the Torah.

This Aggadeta includes a surprising point. In actuality, the law is that one is exempt from sitting in the *succah* if it becomes unbearably hot. So, it is in fact not the gentile nations' leaving that proves their unworthiness but rather their kicking at the *succah* as they leave. Why indeed will they kick at it? Why wouldn't they just walk away?

Our acceptance of the Torah at Mount Sinai played a dual role in our relationship with God. First, it gave us a blueprint for the ideal life, a transcendent life connecting us with God. The recognition of the great good of such a life will form the basis of the gentile nations' complaint in the Messianic era. They will complain about not having had the Torah as a schematic for living it.

There is, however, a second aspect to our covenant to keep God's law.

It expresses our absolute acceptance of Divine providence, the unqualified submission to God and acceptance of His will. Furthermore, we willingly took upon ourselves the role of God's agents throughout history. When we suffered the destruction of Jerusalem and the Temple, bitter exile, murderous Crusades and pogroms or even the Holocaust, we always maintained our faith that God was guiding us towards an ultimate good.

The acceptance of Divine providence is at the heart of the commandment of *succah*, which celebrates God's providence manifest in the Exodus and our miraculous survival in the desert for forty years. The Torah commands (23:42), "You shall dwell in a *succah* for seven days, every citizen of Israel shall dwell in a *succah*." This commandment obliges every Jew to leave his home and move into a *succah* for the duration of the festival; for a week, he constantly reminds himself of God's enveloping providence.

The gentiles who wanted a second chance at the Torah were interested solely in the first aspect of our covenant with God, as a means of connecting with God and being uplifted. They were, however, incapable of submitting to Divine providence and accepting misfortune with absolute faith, and they showed this by kicking at the *succah*, the symbol of providence. They showed themselves unworthy of being the bearers of Torah through history.

vi. Everything Is Everything

EVERYTHING IS A WORD THAT MEANS DIFFERENT THINGS TO different people. How then are we to understand the intent of the Torah when it tells us (*Genesis* 24:1) that "God blessed Abraham with everything (*bakol*)"? There are various interpretations in the Midrash. In fact, according to one opinion, the Torah is referring to a daughter whose name was Kol.

There is also a little known Midrash, quoted by the Vilna Gaon in *Divrei Eliyahu* without source citation, that God gave Abraham the institution of *succah*. The Gaon explains that the Midrash derives this concept from the presentation of the commandment of *succah* (23:42-43), "In booths (*basukkos*) shall you dwell for seven days, every (*kol*) citizen of Israel shall dwell in booths, in order that (*lemaan*) your future generations will know that I established the people of Israel in booths when I brought them forth from the land of Egypt." The acronym formed by the first letters of these three phrases is *bakol*, an allusion to God's blessing to Abraham. How did *succah* represent "everything" to Abraham?

Most people dream of winning the lottery and becoming instant multimillionaires. They imagine that if they had all that money their lives would be transformed and they would enjoy uninterrupted bliss. Studies have shown, however, that quite the opposite is true. In the long run, lottery winners are usually miserable; some even commit suicide. A variety of reasons account for this phenomenon – regret over squandered opportunities, family strife, life-choice confusion and so forth.

All this goes to show us that we cannot really know whether something is beneficial or harmful until the passage of time allows us to view the results with hindsight. We can only evaluate the circumstances or choices of our lives in retrospect, when we have had a chance to assess if they have indeed brought us closer to God. This is the only true and enduring good.

The *succah* connects us to absolute goodness, because it is the symbol of God's providence. It reminds us of the booths in which the Jewish people dwelled in the desert after the Exodus, and according to the Midrash, it also reminds us of the Divine clouds of glory that escorted them throughout those years. The *succah* is, therefore, the symbol of God's benevolent providence.

Because of Abraham's piety and loyalty, God blessed him with the *succah*, in other words, with a specific Divine providence that guided every step of his life and ensured that "everything" that happened to him was for the good, regardless of how it appeared on the surface. Unlike a lottery winner who does not know how his new turn of fortune will play itself out, Abraham knew that "everything" he encountered or experienced would be to his benefit, "everything" was directing him to his destiny as the patriarch of the nation that would redeem all mankind.

vii. Sadducee Agenda

DURING THE SECOND TEMPLE ERA, AN IDEOLOGICAL BATTLE raged between the Rabbis, who upheld the Oral Law, and the Sadducees, who rejected it. The world outlook of the Sadducees was assimilationist, their religious observance lax. The Rambam (*Avos* 1:3) writes that the Sadducees really wanted to reject the Torah altogether, but they felt they had a better chance of success if they did it incrementally. The rejection of the authority of the Oral Law became their fig leaf of justification, the cover-up of their underlying motivation. The Sages of the Talmud recorded only a limited number of their disputes with the Sadducees. It appears they chose those to highlight the Sadducees' corruption — as a closer look at a few of them reveals.

One of the most famous debates regards the date for the proper observance of Shavuos (23:16), "And you shall count for yourselves from after the Sabbath, from the day you bring the *Omer* barley offering, seven full weeks."

The Oral Law interprets "the Sabbath" as the first day of Passover; festivals are also considered Sabbaths in the Torah. Consequently, Shavuos always falls exactly fifty days after the start of Passover. The Sadducees, however, interpret the word Sabbath literally, which means that Shavuos begins forty-nine day from the morrow of the Sabbath following Passover. That is when, they maintained, the *Omer* offering should be brought.

Superficially, this dispute seems to have important practical ramifications but relatively minor philosophical significance. A closer examination uncovers a critical philosophical issue as well. According to the Torah, the Exodus from Egypt was a preliminary stage for the acceptance of the Torah at Mount Sinai fifty days later. But this view was intolerable to the Sadducees, whose Judaism was essentially secular in nature, focusing on nationalism and ethnicity rather than intellectual and spiritual growth.

For the Sadducees, Passover celebrated Jewish national independence not contingent on any subsequent events. The unrelated Shavuos holiday was a national harvest festival. They sought to minimize the calendar connection between Shavuos and Passover by interpreting the verse so that the interlude between them would vary in length from year to year. They rejected the Sages' view of an essentially religious nationalism.

Another dispute that seems philosophically innocuous centered on the incense ritual the Kohen Gadol performed on Yom Kippur. According to the Rabbis, he entered the Holy of Holies with a pan of incense in one hand and a pan of burning coals in the other, pouring the incense onto the coals only after he was inside. The Sadducees contended that he placed the incense on the coals before entering the Holy of Holies. By insisting that the Kohen Gadol be enveloped in a dense cloud of smoke before he entered the Holy of Holies, they symbolically denied the teaching of the Sages that God is intimately involved in the particular affairs of people (*hashgachah pratis*).

The issue of separation, establishing God as more "distant" from man, held a special appeal to the Sadducees, because it gave them more freedom and less accountability in their behavior. This may have been at the root of another dispute. According to the Rabbis, during the festival of Succos, a Kohen poured a water libation on the altar, from where it flowed into drainage ducts and mixed with the regular wine libations. The Talmud (*Succah* 48b) records that the Sadducees rejected this teaching, which is based on the Oral Law.

Rav Tzadok HaKohen, among other rabbinic commentators, finds a deeper significance in the mixing of the water and wine libations. Water is a life-giving substance associated both with the Torah itself and God's kindness (*chessed*). Wine, blood-red in color, suggests strict judgment (*din*). The mixing of wine and water symbolically brings to a close the process of judgment and repentance that begins with Rosh Hashanah and continues through Yom Kippur. By blending the libations we petition God to temper His just effected judgment with His overflowing kindness. Such intense Divine involvement in human affairs, however, was inimical to the Sadducees whose assimilationist agenda preferred a more distant deity.

THE TALMUD (*BERACHOS* 58A) DESCRIBES AN ENCOUNTER between a Sadducee and the blind Rav Sheishess as they await the passage of the king at the roadside. The Sadducee insults Rav Sheishess and ridicules his sightless attempt to greet the king, but Rav Sheishess remains undeterred. On three successive occasions, the Sadducee observes clamorous troops approaching and incorrectly assumes the king is with them. Rav Sheishess, sensing a sudden hush, correctly detects the arrival of the king's entourage and pronounces the appropriate blessing in his presence. The Sadducee, still contemptuous, asks, "How do you bless what you can't see?" The Talmud then wonders about the fate of the obstreperous Sadducee and gives two answers. One view is that his friends put out his eyes, the other is that Rav Sheishess reduced him to a pile of bones.

Why does the Talmud wonder about what happened to the Sadducee? Why should it assume that anything at all happened to him? Apparently, the Talmud sees in this episode allegorical references to the philosophical dispute with the Sadducees. In the story, the Sadducee, who reveres temporal power, feels the Rabbis turn a blind eye to its value and importance, just as Rav Sheishess is literally blind. He scoffs at Rav Sheishess and ridicules his disabilities. Rav Sheishess responds effectively. Imbued with Torah wisdom and perspective, he exhibits the superior understanding of temporal kings, seeing in them a reflection of the glory of the Divine King who appears in a "still thin sound" (*kol demamah dakah*).

Since the story has allegorical overtones, the Talmud inquires about the fate of this Sadducee and, by extension, all Sadducees who misled so many of their Jewish brethren. The answer is God's justice will be done. Either his friends, meaning those led astray by the Sadducees, will eventually come to their senses and turn against him ("put out his eyes"), or the Rabbis themselves will fully demonstrate the hollowness of his views ("reduce him to a pile of bones").

viii. Two Expressions of Joy

JOY IS THE COMMON REQUIREMENT OF ALL THE FESTIVALS, although it is only mentioned specifically in the context of Succos (23:40), "And you shall rejoice before God, your Lord, for seven days." The Talmud enumerates eating meat and drinking wine as expressions of this joy, but of course, the feeling in the heart is paramount. Elsewhere, we find that joy is central to all Torah observance (*Deuteronomy* 28:45-47), "And all these misfortunes shall befall . . . because you did not serve God, your Lord, with joy and satisfaction in all your plenitude."

Languages reflect cultural priorities and interests; Eskimos actually have dozens of terms to tease out the nuances of snow. Hebrew is not particularly concerned with snow, but it has numerous terms for happiness. Most prominent among these are *simchah*, which appears several times in the Torah, and *sason*, which appears once (*Deuteronomy* 28:62). These are the two most frequent expressions of joy that filter through our liturgy.

The Vilna Gaon draws a distinction between these two words. The term *simchah*, he explains, refers to happiness that derives from attaining, whereas *sason* refers to happiness that derives from having.

A close look at the words themselves confirms this distinction. In Hebrew, similar-sounding words formed by changing only one letter are related. Consequently, the root word for *simchah* (*same'ach*, שָׂמֵחַ) is etymologically related to *tzame'ach* (צָמֵחַ), to grow or flourish; the transformation is accomplished by the exchange of the first letter from a *sin* to a *tzaddi*, both of which produce similar lingual sounds. *Simchah*, therefore, portrays happiness derived from activities of growth or attainment.

The root of *sason* is *sass* (שָׂשׂ), twice the letter *sin* (or *shin*), whose numerical value is 300. The numeral 3 is associated with completeness; space consists of three planes, time spans past, present and future, and so on. As such, the letter *shin-sin* expresses completeness in its numerical value, which is a multiple of 3, in the number of digits (3) and even in its three-pronged shape (ש). Along these lines, the Talmud frequently uses the number 300 as an exaggerated expression of size (*Tosaphos*, *Chullin* 95b). The word *sass*, composed of a double *shin-sin*, expresses an intensification of the idea of completeness, of happiness derived from having everything.

These two joys, stemming from becoming and being, encompass the fundamental joyous experiences of man, those experienced as a result of an activity and those that come passively as reflecting a state of being.[4]

---

4. This distinction between becoming and being has important parallels in Jewish thought. Our Sages describe creation as a melding of the Divine expansive desire of kindness (*chessed*) with the restraining quality of judgment (*din*). This concept is expressed in the Divine Name of *Shad-dai* (the One Who Sets Limits). Furthermore, the Torah describes the first six days of creation as "that which God created to do." Our Sages interpret the term "to do" as man's responsibility to complete the work of creation (*tikkun haolam*). This obligation is balanced by the Sabbath, the seventh day of the week, the day of cessation. Its pleasure is a reflective one, not of activity but of being. Finally, Kabbalistic literature sees our approach to God as oscillating between desire (*ratzo*) and ceasing or resting (*shav*).

פרשת בהר
Parashas Behar

i. What Will We Eat?

FOR AN AGRARIAN SOCIETY, THE REQUIREMENT TO LEAVE the land fallow during the *Shemittah* year was a supreme test of faith in providence. The Torah anticipates this anxiety (25:20-21), "And should you say, 'What will we eat in the seventh year since we will not sow nor reap our grain?' Then I will ordain My blessing for you in the sixth year, and it will yield grain for three years. You will sow in the eighth year, but eat from the old grain until the ninth, until the arrival of its grain, you will eat the old."

The Torah predicts people's concerns about the seventh year, yet God answers them concerning the eighth as well. If they would require the bumper crop of the sixth year to provide for the eighth year as well, why wouldn't they express their concern about it?

The answer may be found in a close reading of the words "until the arrival of its grain, you will eat the old (*yashan*)." Elsewhere in the Torah, the term *yashan* carries a precise legal meaning. The Torah forbids Jews living in Israel to eat *chadash*, newly harvested grain from which the *Omer* grain offering has not yet been brought to the Temple. Once the *Omer* was brought, the grain became *yashan* and could be eaten.

In this light, we understand why the Jewish people would not need to worry about the eighth year. Since *Shemittah* observance does not restrict planting in the eighth year, they knew there would be grain available. The only drawback is that before the *Omer* the grain would be *chadash* and prohibited. But if the alternative were starvation, the Torah permits *chadash*. Thus, the people would not express any concern about the eighth year. Nonetheless, God informed them that the blessing of the sixth year would be so great that there would be no need to eat *chadash* in the eighth year; there would plenty of *yashan* left from the sixth year's harvest.

Let us reflect further on this hypothetical question — "What will we eat in the seventh year?" — the Jewish people would ask. It seems they would ask it during planting time in the beginning of the seventh year, when the issue of *Shemittah* is current. How could they be expected to let the land lie fallow, they would complain, if it would lead to starvation?

How can this be? If God promises a harvest in the sixth year bountiful enough to last three years, why would people express any concern? Would they forget their granaries now filled to overflowing?

Earlier, while describing the security people will enjoy when they obey God's will, the Torah states (25:19), "And the land will give forth its produce and you will eat your fill." Rashi comments that the food will be so blessed that a small amount will bring complete satisfaction.

Perhaps this allows us to understand the anxiety of the people in the beginning of the seventh year. Sometimes, the harvest of the sixth year may have been normal, but it still provided three years of nourishment through its supernatural ability to satisfy in small amounts. God reassured the nation that this miraculous aspect of the harvest would endure for three years. With only ordinary grain reserves present as the *Shemittah* year began, the people's anxious questions do not surprise us.

Alternatively, we may suggest that the question of "What will we eat?" could indeed have been asked even after a bumper crop. King Solomon wrote (*Ecclesiastes* 5:9), "One who loves silver is not satisfied with silver." Such is man's weak nature that even when he has enough he continues to "pack away" everything he can. He still imagines he faces the future as if with empty hands. The challenge of the seventh year is to recognize that the extraordinary bumper crop of the sixth year is God's special bounty to enable us to observe the *Shemittah* year without privation.

ii. All Sales Are Not Final

WHEN IT COMES TO REAL ESTATE IN ISRAEL, ALL SALES ARE not final (25:23). "The land shall not be sold in perpetuity, for the land is Mine; for you are sojourners and denizens with Me." The Torah forbids permanent land sales among Jews living in Israel. All lands must be returned, completely free of compensation, to the original owners in the *Yovel* (Jubilee) year, which occurs every fifty years.

What is the purpose of this law? At first glance, it would appear to be for the economic welfare of impoverished sellers; the compulsory land return assures that they or their descendants will not remain landless. A closer examination of the laws governing land sales challenges this assumption.

The Talmud states (*Arachin* 30b) that a buyer of land may not resell the land for two years; presumably, this is to ensure that the holy land is not bandied about like cheap chattel but treated with reverence. Furthermore, the original owner may redeem the land from the buyer even before *Yovel* by returning the purchase money prorated for the amount of time elapsed since the time of the sale.

Elementary economics dictates that any limitation placed on the usage or disposal of property decreases its value. For example, a property in midtown Manhattan would drop in value precipitously if restrictions of building more than six stories up were imposed. In the case of a landowner in Israel as well, the restrictions on resale and the owner's right to redeem his land make the property less attractive to buyers and, consequently, drive down the price. Clearly, these laws are not for the economic protection or benefit of impoverished landowners. What then is their purpose?

Apparently, the Torah wants to insure that the land remains in the families of the original conquerors who crossed the Jordan with Joshua. In this way, the land itself will always be an ancestral reminder of God's providence in taking the Jewish nation from Egypt and bringing them into the Holy Land. The purpose of the law is not for the benefit of the seller or the buyer. It is to establish the identity of the true Owner of the land, and to make us aware that all of us are no more than "sojourners and denizens" whose presence on it reflects His providential hand in history.[1]

---

1. A similar concept applies to the specific prohibition against boundary encroachment, which is operative only in the land of Israel.

פרשת בחקותי
Parashas Bechukosai

i. There Is No Happenstance

THERE IS ONE UNDERLYING CAUSE FOR ALL THE PUNISHments that will befall the Jewish people (26:21), "If you behave toward Me with happenstance and refuse to heed Me."

The minor misfortunes we encounter in our lives can be messages from God reminding us to repent and return to Him. The bounty enjoyed by the faithful and pious is God's sign of approval, as He promises (*Deuteronomy* 11:13-21) in the second paragraph of the *Shema*. But if we see all events as mere happenstance, we disassociate ourselves from His providential guidance. Then God uses greater calamities to get our attention and bring us to our senses.

The very last Mishnah of the Talmud states that God will grant every righteous person three hundred and ten worlds, as it is written (*Proverbs* 8:21), "To bequeath existence (*yeish*) to those who love Me, and I will fill their storehouses." The numerical value of the promised *yeish* (יֵשׁ) is three hundred and ten. The Hebrew word for gift, *shai* (שַׁי), spelled with the same letters, has the identical numerical value.

The Mishnah conveys a profound concept. The word *yeish*, in this context, means existence, which can be either necessary or unnecessary. In fact, our temporal existences are really unnecessary. No one's inherent nature absolutely requires that he must exist. Our very existence is thus a gift God grants us for the purpose and privilege of having a relationship with Him, the Source of existence. The reward (*shai*) of the righteous is to gain an eternal existence (*yeish*) through clinging to God.

The word for happenstance is *keri* (קֶרִי), which also has a numerical value of three hundred and ten. Since there is no happenstance in the holy language, we may assume there is a connection. In fact, *keri* is the flip side of *yeish*. A *baal keri* is one who has spent his seed and, by extension, his potential. People who "behave with happenstance" live without true existence, because they do not see God's presence. They are the diametric opposites of those who connect themselves to God and thereby find existence, as symbolized by the three hundred and ten worlds of *yeish*.

ii. Two Couples

OUR THRICE-DAILY *SHEMONEH ESREI* (EIGHTEEN BLESSINGS) prayer originally contained only eighteen blessings, as evidenced by its name. Later, the Sages added a supplementary blessing called *"Velamalshinim,"* which asks for the downfall of Jewish apostates, and inserted it after the twelfth blessing. Unlike the prior blessings, this supplementary blessing begins with "and" (the conjunctive *vav*), apparently coupling it to the prior blessing. One might have thought that the "and" is there because it is an added blessing. One blessing later, however, yet another blessing, *"Veliy'rushalayim,"* begins with the conjunctive *vav*; in it, we ask for God's return to Jerusalem. No other blessing starts with a conjunction.

Why did the Sages begin just these two blessings with conjunctions?

In the blessing immediately before the prayer regarding the apostates, we petition God for the return of upstanding judges to administer His Divine justice. Perhaps our Sages wished to indicate that it is not vengeful hatred that drives our prayers concerning the apostates. In fact, we do not arrogate to ourselves to judge others unless God has blessed and enlightened us to be His agents of justice in this important matter.

In the next couplet, we join the petition for God's return to Jerusalem to the preceding blessing on behalf of the righteous. What stands in the way of God's return? Why does God turn away from us? We find the answer in the reproofs of the lengthy *Tochachah* (26:27-28), "And if in spite of all this you do not listen to Me, and you walk with Me with happenstance, then I will walk with you with enraged happenstance." Happenstance is the opposite of providence. If the Jewish nation ignores God's providential messages, then God will remove His manifest providence from them and leave them to the vicissitudes of exile. The end of the exile for which we pray in the fifteenth blessing can only be accomplished by the fulfillment of the fourteenth blessing, the ascendancy of the righteous who live by their faith (*tzaddik b'emunaso yichyeh*). The presence of cognate forms of the words righteousness (*tzedek*) and trust (*bitachon*), three of each, in this short blessing underscores this theme.

The coupling of these two blessings reveals the spine of Jewish history. God places signposts, roadblocks, stoplights and other markers along the pathways of history to guide us to our final destiny. If we ignore God's directives as if they were happenstance, we will wander endlessly without nearing our ultimate goal. The righteous, guided by the God's directions, guarantee history's dénouement, God's return and Jerusalem's rebuilding. Their faith leads the nation and will usher in God's return to Jerusalem.

iii. *Joyless Festivals in Israel*

RABBI YOCHANAN, WHO LIVED IN ISRAEL ABOUT TWO HUNdred years after the destruction of the Second Temple, was in close contact with the Jewish communities of Babylon. As quoted in the Talmud (*Shabbos* 145b), he wonders why the festivals are more joyous in Babylon than in Israel. And he offers a solution based on the Prophets.

Hosea prophesied (2:13), "I shall end all her joy, her festive gatherings, her new months, her Sabbaths and her festivals." Isaiah prophesied (1:14), "My soul despises your new months and holidays; they have become a burden to Me." Both prophets conveyed that there is a specific curse regarding festivals in the land of Israel.

What did Isaiah mean by "they have become a burden to Me"? Rabbi Elazar comments, "It is not enough for Israel that they sinned before Me, but they also burdened Me to determine which harsh decree I shall bring upon them." The Talmud concludes that this "burden," clearly just an anthropomorphism, causes more frequent troubles and a general diminution of joy during the festivals in Israel.

Many questions come to mind. Why was the land of Israel singled out for a harsher decree long after the destruction of the Temple, when only a fraction of the Jewish people remained there? In what way is it a greater "burden" for God to make harsh decrees in the land of Israel? How do we define this additional sin of "burdening" God over and above the sins that lead to Divine retribution in the first place? And how does this sin relate to the festivals?

The most essential aspect of the festivals is to reinforce the idea of God's continual benevolence and providence; they recall the redemption from Egypt (Passover), the giving of the Torah (Shavuos) and God's providence during the forty years in the desert (Succos). This providence is most manifest in the land of Israel, as we read in the second paragraph of the *Shema* prayer. It is there that man can achieve the closest possible relationship with the Creator.

It stands to reason that the land of Israel demands a "reverse providence" when it is not fulfilling its purpose, and so, "bad" things tend to happen in Israel. This is especially true during the festivals when, in good times, the great gathering at the Temple would have reverberated with paeans to His providence. Now, as the Temple lies in ruins, the people are banished and silence greets the festivals, it is fitting that the absence of providence be most acutely felt.

Ideally, God wants people to choose good for its own sake, without prodding by miraculous occurrences. But people tend to be wayward, and God redirects nature to produce providential events that guide them back on the right path. The Talmud characterizes this active override of the laws of nature as a "burden" on God's ultimate plan. If all that is required is a small providential nudge then the "burden" is considered small, but if a major calamity is needed in order to get their attention, they are imposing a great "burden," so to speak, on God's plan for the world.

People living in the land of Israel, the place designated for the most manifest providence, are held to a higher standard. For them, small nudges were often not enough. They required more significant intervention and thereby caused an additional "burden." And during the festivals, when the "reverse providence" was so manifest, the "burden" was the greatest.

iv. *A Fitting Cadence*

THE BOOK OF LEVITICUS BEGINS WITH GOD'S CALL TO Moses to initiate the Divine service and comes to a disturbing climax with the *Tochachah,* the dire warnings of Divine retribution should the people go astray. It is a fitting place to turn the last page and open the next Book. But surprisingly, a few didactic laws regarding animals sanctified for the Divine service follow the dramatic *Tochachah.* Why do these laws appear here? The anticlimactic conclusion diminishes the power of the reproof, distracts from the Book's theme and detracts from its message.

The very last passage of Leviticus discusses the laws of *temurah*, among the laws of other holy items. An animal sanctified as an offering cannot be exchanged for another. If the exchange is attempted, both animals remain in the holy domain. The Torah repeatedly stresses (27:33) that no distinction be made "between good and bad." The laws of this section teach that once an object attains holiness it must remain so unless properly redeemed.

Upon consideration, this law provides a fitting metaphor for the consolation that concludes the *Tochachah,* where God declares (25:24), "Even in the land of their enemies I will not cast them away, nor will I loathe them to destroy them and void My covenant with them." We see this promise etched into the structure of *halachah* in the laws of *temurah* and other holy items. God has invested the Jewish people with sanctity by selecting them. Whether "good or bad," they cannot be exchanged or lose their higher designation. They, too, will have redemption.

במדבר
NUMBERS

פרשת במדבר
Parashas Bamidbar

i. Statistics Tell the Story

STATISTICS ARE EASY TO OVERLOOK, BUT UPON CLOSER inspection, they often tell an interesting story. The Torah gives us a tribe by tribe breakdown of the population figures for the Jewish people in the desert. If we organize the tribes according to size, the most populous is Judah, and the least populous are Benjamin, Menasheh, Ephraim and Levi, each being smaller than Judah (see chart on next page). Can we explain this large difference in the rates of population growth?

Let us first consider Levi, the smallest of the tribes. With Levi the discrepancy is actually even larger than it appears. The count of 22,300 for Levi includes all males from one-month-old infants and up, while the counts for the other tribes include only males between the ages of 20 and 60. Had the Torah counted Levi according to this yardstick, their count would have been considerably smaller and the discrepancy with the other tribes considerably larger.

TRIBE	AFTER EXODUS	40 YEARS LATER	TRIBE	AFTER EXODUS	40 YEARS LATER
Judah	74,600	76,500	Gad	45,650	40,500
Dan	62,700	64,400	Asher	41,500	53,400
Shimon	59,300	22,200	Ephraim	40,500	32,500
Zebulun	57,400	60,500	Benjamin	35,400	45,600
Yissachar	54,400	64,300	Menasheh	32,500	52,700
Naphtali	53,400	45,400	Total	603,550	601,730
Reuven	46,500	43,730	(Levi	22,000	23,000)

This anomaly dovetails well with the Midrashic tradition that the Egyptians, because of their superstitious fears of persecuting a priestly caste, did not enslave the tribe of Levi. Jacob had designated the Levites from the very beginning as a priestly caste with regard to national Torah instruction. (They did not, however, replace the firstborn as the priestly caste with regard to performing the Divine service until after the sin of the Golden Calf.) The Torah attributes the rapid growth of the Jewish people to the Egyptian oppression (*Exodus* 1:7), "Just as [the Egyptians] afflicted [the Jewish people] so did they increase." It follows that the Levites, who were not afflicted, did not multiply as rapidly.

Interestingly, among the enslaved tribes, the three tribes descended from Rachel — Ephraim, Benjamin and Menasheh — have the smallest counts. Can we account for this coincidence?

The Midrash states (*Pirkei d'Rabbi Eliezer* 48) that the tribe of Ephraim tried to leave Egypt thirty years prior to the Exodus. Jacob and Joseph had both prophesied that God would surely redeem the Jewish people (*Genesis* 50:24), but the people of Ephraim couldn't wait. Unfortunately, they met with a terrible disaster when they clashed with the Philistines, and some 200,000 died on the battlefield.

Let us make a simple calculation. Since Ephraim numbered 40,500 at the time of the Exodus thirty years later, they would have numbered more than 300,000, estimating conservatively, had they not made that first ill-advised attempt to escape. This is puzzling. Why would Ephraim have been so much larger than any other tribe, over four times as large as Judah, the largest of the tribes?

It seems likely that Ephraim's premature attempt to gain freedom captured the imagination of the other tribes as well and that substantial elements accompanied them. The largest single group among the 200,000 casualties was undoubtedly from Ephraim, but it is likely that the majority of the casualties were from all the other tribes combined; had they not made a break for freedom, the 200,000 who would have been spared death, instead of entirely swelling the ranks of Ephraim, would have been distributed among all the tribes.

Now let us consider which among the other tribes were most likely to have joined Ephraim's campaign to hasten the redemption. The most likely candidates would be Benjamin and Menasheh, the tribes most closely related to Ephraim by virtue of common descent from Rachel. Consequently, these three tribes would have had the largest contingents in the escape group, and they would also have proportionately suffered the highest casualties. It is no wonder they were the smallest of the tribes.

One might have expected Ephraim, the leader of the rebels leaving Egypt, to have the most casualties and, consequently, the smallest population. Nonetheless, although they probably did suffer higher casualties, their original population base was disproportionately larger because both Jacob and Joseph had blessed them to be fruitful. Therefore, despite their decimation on the battlefield, they remained somewhat larger than their two main partners.

At the other end of the spectrum, we find Judah, with the largest population. While some members of the tribe of Judah may have also joined the rebels, their numbers were relatively small. Why? Before his death, Jacob had predicted and promoted Judah's future role as leader of the Jewish people. Leadership can express itself equally in restraint and patience as in courageous action. The tribe of Judah, having largely spurned Ephraim's premature call to exodus, did not suffer heavy casualties, leaving them with the highest population figures among the tribes.

The population chart reveals another statistical quirk — the precipitous drop by nearly two-thirds (59,000 to 22,000) in the population of the tribe of Shimon. This can be explained by the debacle with the Moabite women in the fortieth year in the desert. The Torah reports that 24,000 perished by Divine wrath in the ensuing plague. The Torah further reports that Moses established courts to judge and execute those who had participated in the concurrent idolatrous rites. The Talmud states that there were 88,000 courts, each of which executed 2 people. The total number of deaths resulting from all these calamities was about 200,000.

Since a prince from the tribe of Shimon initiated the debauchery with the Moabite women, we can reasonably assume that his tribe participated disproportionately and suffered the disproportionate losses, as reflected in the final population figures.

ii. Numbers in Reverse

After the sin of the Golden Calf, God relieved the firstborn of their duties in the performance of the Divine service and replaced them with the tribe of Levi; the substitution of each individual firstborn by a Levite released him from his obligations.

The exchange was almost exactly one for one. There were 22,273 firstborn and 22,000 Levites. There remained 273 firstborn for whom there were no substitute Levites. A lottery determined the identity of these 273, and their redemption was monetary, five *shekalim* each (3:49-50). "Moses took the redemption money from those remaining after the redemption of the Levites. He took the money from the firstborn of the people of Israel — five, sixty, three hundred and one thousand *shekalim*."

Ordinarily, the Torah gives large irregular numbers in descending order of their components, first thousands, then hundreds, then tens, then units. For instance, the population count of the tribe of Gad, which was 45,650, is given as 45,000, 600 and 50 rather than 50, 600 and 45,000. Yet when the Torah calculates the total redemption money as 1,365 *shekalim*, it gives the components in ascending order — 5, 60, 300 and 1,000.

This reversal signals a significance in the number itself. When the Torah (*Genesis* 32:1) gives Sarah's life span in reverse order — 7, 20 and 100 years — our Sages deduce important information about the various stages of her life. The reverse listing of the redemption money likewise signals significance. Similarly, the Torah gives the count of the firstborn as 22,000, 3, 70 and 200. Although the Torah lists the thousand component first, as expected, it enumerates the additional 273 in reverse order. Clearly, the Torah is calling attention to this number and the 1,365 *shekalim* that resulted. What is the significance?

Upon reflection, both 365 and 1,000 are meaningful and related numbers. There are 365 days in the solar year and 365 prohibitions in the Torah, a sign of totality and completeness. The Hebrew word for the number 1,000 is *eleph* (אֶלֶף), which can also mean "to teach" (אַלֵּף). The combination of these two concepts indicates that the Levites were already Divinely designated in Egypt as the perpetual teachers of the Jewish people; their numbers reflected it.

פרשת נשא

Parashas Naso

i. Tithes and the Unfaithful Wife

WHAT MIGHT CAUSE A WOMAN TO BE UNFAITHFUL TO HER husband? The Torah provides a hint (5:9-12). "And every portion from any of the sanctified portions that the people of Israel bring to the Kohen shall be his. A man's sanctified portions shall be his, and what a man gives to the Kohen shall be his. God spoke to Moses saying, 'Speak to the people of Israel and say to them: Any man whose wife shall go astray and be unfaithful to him . . .' "

The laws concerning an unfaithful wife immediately follow the law obliging one to give his tithes to the Kohanim. The Talmud (*Berachos* 63a) notes this juxtaposition and states, "If you ignore your obligation to bring the tithes to the Kohen, by your life, you'll come to him with your unfaithful wife."

How are we to understand the Talmud's reasoning? Are our Sages suggesting that Divine providence would direct an innocent woman to acts that arouse suspicions of faithlessness? Why should a woman suffer the indignities of suspected faithlessness just because her husband neglected to give tithes to the Kohen? Rather, we must infer a natural rather than a providential connection between these events. How is this so?

Psychologically speaking, the phenomenon of an unfaithful wife is odd. Our Sages see home and marriage as central to a woman's personality, more so than for a man; in the Talmud, the Rabbis refer to their wives as their "homes." It is the woman who lights Sabbath candles and ushers the holy day of peace and tranquility into the home. According to the Talmud (*Kiddushin* 41a), a woman has a stronger natural imperative to marry than does a man. "It is better to live with any companion than to live alone (*tav lemeisav tan du milemeisav armelu*)," declares Reish Lakish with regard to a woman's attitude to marriage; this observation of Reish Lakish has legal ramifications. Men, however, do not feel this as strongly. Perhaps this is because God created Adam independent, while Eve was created as his companion. Marriage, companionship, the home, these are the underpinnings of a woman's life. Why risk them by being unfaithful?

Rabbi Eliyahu Dessler, in his work *Michtav MeEliyahu*, explains that love begins with giving. In fact, the very word "to love," *ahav* (אהב), contains the two-letter word "to give," *hav* (הב). True love blooms as we give of ourselves to others; in so doing, we extend the primary love we have for ourselves onto those to whom we give. The command to love one's neighbor as oneself stems from this reality.

For a woman to feel secure in her home and marriage, she must view her husband as a giving and loving person. If, however, her husband is selfish and ungiving, she feels alone, tortured by the form of companionship without its substance. In this case, she is at risk of being unfaithful to her husband as she seeks to fill her void.

This is what the juxtaposition of tithes and the unfaithful woman tells us. A person's failure to bring tithes to the Kohen is a sign of an abiding selfishness that will not cease at the threshold of his home. This man will undoubtedly treat his wife with selfishness and indifference. His will be a loveless home. In this context, thoughts of infidelity will cross his wife's mind. In the end, he will have to face the very Kohen to whom he failed to give his tithes.

ii. More on Marriage

AT CIRCUMCISIONS, THERE IS A VENERABLE CUSTOM FOR ALL the assembled to say to the newborn, "Just as you have entered the covenant, so too may you enter into Torah, marriage and good deeds." Why do we mention these three milestones in a person's life, and why in this particular order? It cannot be chronological, because good deeds should and would come before marriage.

Let us consider a famous saying by Simon the Just (*Pirkei Avos* 1:2), "The world is supported by three things — Torah, Divine service (*avodah*) and acts of kindness (*gemilus chassadim*)." There is a striking parallel between this statement and the blessing we give a just circumcised boy. Torah and good deeds are the same in both sets of three, and as we shall see, marriage parallels Divine service on several levels. Perhaps our customary liturgy intends to mirror the three pillars that support the world.

The essential element of Divine service is self-sacrifice and submission, the sublimation of the self in the greater act of worshiping God. Marriage also places a lifelong demand upon each partner to restrain his or her own desires and inclinations in order to accommodate the other. If this is done in the interest of forming a harmonious union dedicated to the service of God, then the marriage mirrors Divine service. Even our devotion to our children cannot match this element of sacrifice in the spousal relationship, since our natural love for children is actually an extension of our own self-love.

On a deeper level, the purpose of a Jewish marriage is to build a home that is a minor sanctuary, as the Talmud (*Sotah* 17a) states, "When a man and a woman marry, if they are worthy the Divine Presence dwells with them." In this sense, the spiritual construction of such a home and all that goes on within is Divine service of the highest order.

We may further add that the three pillars and the corresponding milestones of life are related to the lower three levels of the soul. The intellectual study of Torah relates to the *neshamah*, the emotional service of marriage to the *ruach* and the physical good deeds to the *nefesh*. Thus, the three blessings we give the newborn mirror the pillars of the world and the descending realms of the soul. It is a momentous blessing appropriate for the solemn occasion of entry into the covenant of Abraham.

iii. The Suspected Adulteress

THE SUSPECTED ADULTERESS WAS TESTED IN A SUPERNATURAL fashion. The Kohen wrote the ineffable Name of God on a piece of paper and dissolved it in a beaker of water. Then (5:27-28), "[the Kohen] shall give her the water to drink, and if she was defiled and unfaithful to her husband, the curse-bearing waters shall come into her for bitterness and her belly shall become distended, her thigh shall shrivel, and the woman shall become a curse word among her people."

This verse describes the effects of the water in proper sequence. The water passes into the stomach of the adulteress first and distends her belly. Then it passes lower into the thigh and causes it to "fall," ultimately killing her. Earlier, the Torah instructs the Kohen to warn the suspected adulteress in the reverse order (5:21), "God will make you into a curse word and an oath among your people, when God causes your thigh to fall and your belly to become distended." The Talmud (*Sotah* 9b) explains that the warning, measure for measure, follows the pattern of the sin. She "began with the thigh," a euphemism for her carnal desire, therefore her thigh is cursed first. The punishment then proceeds in the order the waters naturally course through her body, top to bottom.

Further consideration of the procedure reveals other fitting elements in this Divinely effected punishment. The distended belly suggests an artificial rapid pregnancy, pseudocyeisis. Her punishment shows that her act of passion and transgression could result in a vain, worse than worthless pregnancy; it could have produced a *mamzer*, an illegitimate outcast whose descendants are forevermore forbidden to marry into legitimate society.

The dissolved Name of God is the catalyst for her examination. Her death suggests that God's presence cannot abide in a woman whose prurient pursuits lead her to betray the trust of her husband and violate the sanctity of the home, the cornerstone of Jewish life.

פרשת בהעלותך
Parashas Beha'aloscha

i. Protected by Beams

THE CLOUDS OF GLORY THAT ESCORTED THE JEWISH NATION through the desert for forty years regularly changed their appearance. According to Rashi, they formed a beamed roof (*korah*) when they traveled and a temporary porous structure (*succah*) when they encamped.

One would have expected that a beamed roof, which conjures up an image of a more permanent structure, would hover above when the people encamped and the temporary form would appear when they traveled. Surprisingly, the reverse was the case. How do we account for this?

When a person travels, he leaves behind the safety of his home and faces the perils of capricious nature and malicious man. This can adversely affect wealth, health and reputation (see *Rashi* on *Genesis* 12:2). In these circumstances, God's unseen providential hand overrides the laws of nature more frequently in order to provide protection. Fittingly, Rashi refers to the providential clouds of glory as the more protective beam when the Jewish nation traveled. It was precisely then that the Jewish people required stronger metaphysical protection.

ii. *The Missing Tastes*

WHAT MORE WOULD IT TAKE TO SATISFY THE JEWISH PEOPLE? God rained down on them manna from the heavens, the food of the angels. They did not have to work for it or pay for it. It was delicious and filling, and according to the Midrash, the person eating it could will it to have any taste in the world. And yet, after only one year, three days distant from Mount Sinai, some of the people tired of the manna and wistfully recalled the foods they had enjoyed in Egypt (11:4ff).

According to the *Sifrei* (87), there were five tastes the manna could not assume — cucumbers, melons, leeks, onions and garlic. And these were precisely the five foods they had enjoyed in Egypt and about whose absence they were now complaining (11:5). The Midrash explains that these foods are harmful to a pregnancy. It would seem that the exclusion of these foods also had a symbolic value for the Jewish people. Just as the fetus passes through a forty-week period of gestation in the womb before birth, so too would the Jewish people pass through a forty-year period of national development in the desert before they could enter the holy land. God would not allow the manna to take the form of a food harmful to a woman's pregnancy and, by symbolic extension, to development of the nation.

Granted that five foods were excluded from the taste of the manna, we may still wonder if this was so great a loss to deserve such strenuous complaints. What was really bothering the Jewish people? The clue lies in another complaint they voiced at the time (11:5), "We miss the fish we ate in Egypt for nothing." The *Sifrei* notes the curious words "for nothing" and wonders if in fact the inhospitable Egyptians provided free fish to the enslaved Jews. The answer, concludes the *Sifrei,* is that the Jews were longing "for nothing," for their former hedonistic lifestyle, unencumbered by God's commands. The manna represented the limiting and channeling of physical desires. They wanted to be free of restrictions.

In response to this rebellious group, God sent innumerable birds called *slav*, so many that (11:20) "it would come out of your nostrils." And what did this mysterious *slav* bird taste like? In one brief phrase, the Torah states that "the *slav* will be strange (*zara,* זָרָא)." The *Baal HaTurim* comments on the unusual spelling of the word *zara*, which ends with the letter *aleph* instead of the usual *hei*. He states that the *aleph*, whose numerical value is 1, indicates that the *slav* had the capacity to taste like every possible food except one. Apparently, the *aleph* replacing the *hei*, which has a numerical value of 5, indicates that instead of lacking five tastes like the manna, the *slav* lacked only one. Which was this elusive taste? The *Baal HaTurim* identifies it as the Leviathan.

The Leviathan, according to the Midrash, is the mammoth beast created on the sixth day, which God immediately killed and salted away as a reward for the righteous in the next world. The *slav*, which lacked the taste of the Leviathan, represented the unbridled pursuit of material desires with no aspect of spirituality. Its inability to metamorphose into the taste of the Leviathan indicated that when man succumbs to total materialism he loses the opportunity of gaining eternal life for his soul.

The manna, on the other hand, entailed numerous commandments, instructed the nation in Divine providence and gave the Jewish people access to the eternal spiritual world. A shortage of five tastes was but a small price to pay for such immense reward.

iii. Complainers and Cravers

NOWHERE ELSE IN THE TORAH IS THERE ANYTHING LIKE THE two inverted letters (*nuns*) that appear in this *parashah*. They flank the famous couplet (10:35-36), "And it came to pass when the Ark journeyed, Moses said, 'Arise, O God, and let Your foes be scattered, let those who hate You flee before You.' And when it rested he would say, 'Reside tranquilly, O God, among the myriad thousands of Israel.' " What is the significance of these verses being bracketed by the inverted letters?

The Talmud (*Shabbos* 116a) explains that these inverted letters serve as a separation between two incidents of *puranius*, failings of the Jewish people in the desert. Before we take a closer look at this explanation, let us briefly summarize the sequence of the relevant verses.

First, the Torah describes the Jewish people leaving Mount Sinai. Then, an inverted letter *nun* appears. Next come the two verses in which Moses describes the Ark's journeys and restings. Then another inverted letter *nun* appears. Then (11:1-4), "The people were like complainers, evil in God's ears, and God heard, and His anger flared, and God's fire burned among them and consumed the corner of the encampment. And the people cried out to Moses, and Moses prayed to God, and the fire subsided . . . The rabble among them felt a craving . . . and they said, 'Who will feed us meat?' "

A question arises. Where do we see two failings bracketing the inverted letters? Two consecutive failings immediately follow the inverted letters, the complainers (*mis'onenim*) and the cravers (*mis'avim*), but it appears that none precedes them, only the seemingly innocuous breaking of camp at Mount Sinai and the beginning of the journey.

Rashi resolves this problem by stating that the craving for meat began at Sinai but was not verbalized until after the incident of the complainers. The Tosaphists disagree with Rashi, perhaps because there is no indication of a latent craving in the verses prior to their travel. The inverted letters, in their opinion, should separate between recorded failings; the verses with their inverted *nuns* should have been placed between the actual incidents of the complainers and the cravers rather than after the unrecorded desire for meat. The Tosaphists suggest instead that the first failing was the very departure from Sinai, which was too eager, "like children scampering from school at the bell."

Questions are raised by the explanation of the Tosaphists as well. If the two failings are the hasty departure and the complainers, why isn't there another divider between the complainers and the cravers? More fundamentally, why indeed should the Torah separate between two failings? In fact, there are consecutive failings in the Book of *Exodus* (15:23-16:3) with no intervening markings. Apparently, the Torah has no general requirement to separate failings. Why then do these two particular events demand separation?

If we look carefully at the verses, we notice that the Torah does not tell us the nature of the complainers' complaint. We may suggest it was about their actual journey from Sinai. While the Jewish people encamped at the foot of Mount Sinai, they led a charmed life of Torah study unencumbered by the mundane cares, responsibilities and challenges they would face in the land of Israel. Perhaps, to some degree, they resisted and retreated from the new challenges that entry into the land would create. Furthermore, they may have wanted to remain in an atmosphere of pure spirituality. But in fact, God does not want all of Israel, as a nation, to withdraw from the world. He wants us to engage and elevate it.

At the other end of the spectrum stood the cravers, driven by material desires long repressed in the sheltered environment of Sinai. Once the journey began, they anticipated a return to a normal lifestyle in Israel. Their desires resurfaced, and they cried out for meat.

Thus, the departure from Sinai set in motions two unfortunate chains of events in opposite directions. Those who could not bear to leave the atmosphere of pure spirituality became the complainers. At the other extreme were those whose desires became inflamed at the prospect of entering the land; they became the cravers.

A human being faces challenges from opposite directions. If his materialistic side is overly stimulated, it may spring up to haunt him. If he does not have the proper guidance to determine his own role and place in the service of God, he may leave his obligations unfulfilled. The antidote, bracketed by the inverted letters, is the constant accompaniment of the Holy Ark of the Torah. The bracketed verses teach that the Torah must accompany the people when they travel, in other words, whatever path they take as they "leave from Sinai". So too should it accompany them when they rest, as represented by the yearlong stay at Sinai. The Torah provides each person with the proper balance for him or her.

The numerical value of two inverted *nuns*, each having a value of 50, totals 100, the number that symbolizes perfection in Kabbalistic literature. The unique inverted *nuns* teach us a vital lesson. The way to navigate the middle ground between asceticism and materialism is by holding on to the Torah. It is the golden mean to perfection in this world for the next.

iv. *Moses, Rouser of the Rabble*

MOST OF THE TROUBLES IN THE DESERT CAN BE TRACED TO the *eiruv rav*, the Egyptian rabble that accompanied the Jewish people in the Exodus. In this *parashah*, we again encounter them under the name *asafsuf* (אֲסַפְסֻף), identified as the *eiruv rav* according to *Targum Onkelos* (11:4). "The rabble (אֲסַפְסֻף) among them felt a craving . . . and they said, 'Who will feed us meat?' "

According to the Midrash (*Shemos Rabbah* 42:6), Moses petitioned God to allow the Egyptian rabble who wished to convert to join the Jewish exodus from Egypt. God did not endorse this idea, nor did He absolutely forbid it. He left it up to Moses, who decided to include them.

Why did Moses include the rabble despite God's tacit disapproval? And why didn't God explicitly forbid Moses to take them along if it would harm the Jewish people?

Moses loved God and all of mankind as reflections of the Divine image with the fullest measure of his soul. He wanted all the world to share in the knowledge of God. He knew that the ultimate goal of history is to imbue all mankind with the same transcendent knowledge and love of God that resonated in the depths of his soul. Moses wanted to expedite history by embracing the Egyptian rabble who sought conversion.

But God counseled Moses that he sought too much. The great multitude of converts did not share the historical experience of the Jewish nation, nor would they identify equally with the patriarchs to whom they were not related by blood. Smaller numbers of converts could be absorbed, but such a large group were most likely to prove indigestible.

Moses, driven by his love of God, nonetheless pursued his noble goal. After all, mankind has free choice, and Moses took it upon himself to raise the converts to the level of the Jewish people. Unfortunately, he was not successful, and time and again, the rabble rebelled against God and caused others to sin as well. In fact, their complaints in this incident caused Moses to declare to God that he was overwhelmed. The ensuing events led to the prophecy of Eldad and Meidad, which according to the Midrash was that Moses would not enter the land.

In a subtle manner, the Torah draws a connecting thread between the *asafsuf* and the incident of the spies, which happened soon afterward and prevented the nation from entering the land. In *Parashas Beha'aloscha,* the term *asaf* (אָסַף) appears ten times in various cognate forms and contexts. Immediately afterwards, *Parashas Shelach* recounts the story of the ten spies who slandered the land of Israel, and the word *eidah* (עֵדָה), which means group or congregation, appears ten times. Moses, in fact, calls the ten slandering spies an *eidah ra*, an evil congregation. Thus, the Torah makes an implicit correlation between the ten spies and the rabble who brought catastrophe on the Jewish people.

Perhaps we may suggest that the name *asafsuf* is a contraction of *asaf asaf*, an allusion to the circumstances of their joining the Jewish nation. *Asaf*, which means to gather, indicates that Moses gathered in the potential Egyptian converts. God demurred. Moses persisted. For better and mostly for worse, he then gathered them fully into the nation, so that in the end they were, so to speak, doubly gathered.

v. *Eldad and Meidad*

ELDAD AND MEIDAD. THE ALLITERATIVE SOUND CLOTHES the names in an aura of artificiality, as if they carry a hidden message (11:26). "Two men remained behind in the camp, the name of one was Eldad, the name of the other Meidad, and the spirit rested upon them; they had been among the recorded ones but had not gone out to the tent, and they prophesied in the camp."

The Torah draws further attention to the names by stating that "the name of one was Eldad, the name of the other Meidad." Ordinarily, the Torah mentions people by name without specifically stating "his name was such and such." It may be that Eldad and Meidad were their actual names, but the Torah records them in a way that suggests a greater significance. What might that be?

Let us consider: How did Eldad and Meidad come on the scene? Three days earlier, the people left Mount Sinai. A series of unfortunate events culminated in their listening to the spies and having to remain in the desert for fully forty years. The first was the complainers (*mis'onenim*), followed by the insurrection of the rabble (*asafsuf*) who craved meat and beleaguered Moses for it.

Moses, feeling set upon, complained to God (11:11-14), "Why have I not found favor in Your eyes that You placed the burden of this entire people upon me? Did I conceive this entire people or did I give birth to it, that You should say to me, 'Carry them in your bosom, as a nurse carries a suckling infant, to the land You promised their forefathers'? . . . I cannot carry this entire nation alone, for it is too heavy for me!"

God responded by instituting a council of seventy elders to provide additional conduits for prophecy. According to the Midrash, Moses selected six elders from each tribe, for a total of seventy-two, two more than a normal high court, and then excluded two by lottery — Eldad and Meidad. According to the Talmud (*Sanhedrin* 17a), they remained in the camp nonetheless and prophesied, predicting that Moses would die and Joshua would lead the people into Israel. We find a suggestion of the catastrophic and offensive nature of their prophecy in Joshua's visceral response, "My lord Moses, destroy them."

Now, we can perhaps gain new insight into the names Eldad and Meidad. The word *dad* in Hebrew means breast. Eldad, therefore, means "to the bosom" and Meidad means "from the bosom." Together, they evoke an implicit prophetic response to Moses' complaint about being wet nurse to the people. The complaints originated from the rabble Moses had brought along, despite God's warning that he was biting off more than he could chew. And now Moses was feeling overwhelmed by his task. God would indeed remove his role as wet nurse from him. The two "dads," however, prophesied that he would not bring the people into the land.[1]

vi. *Joshua Had No Sons*

JOSHUA MEANT WELL, BUT OUR SAGES CRITICIZED HIM FOR his impulsive response (11:27-28). "The youth ran and told Moses, and he said, 'Eldad and Meidad are prophesying in the camp.' Joshua, son of Nun, the servant of Moses from his youth, spoke up and said, 'My lord Moses, destroy them.' "

According to the *Sifrei* (75-96) and the Talmud (*Sanhedrin* 17a), Eldad and Meidad prophesied that Moses would die before entering Israel and that Joshua would bring the people into the land. Joshua felt this was an affront to Moses, and he sprang to his defense.

But he shouldn't have, at least not in this way. By declaring that Eldad and Meidad deserved the death sentence, Joshua preempted Moses' prerogative as preeminent teacher of the generation. The Talmud (*Eruvin* 63b) notes that the genealogy of the Book of Chronicles lists Joshua as having no male descendants, a sign of Divine displeasure for someone in his position. The Talmud suggests that his offering a legal opinion in front of his teacher Moses caused it.

1. The first hint of a decree barring Moses from the land appears when Pharaoh increases the oppression of the people and Moses asks God (*Exodus* 6:1; *Rashi*), "Why did you harm the people?" God responds, "Now you will see My salvation." The Midrash comments that Moses would see God's salvation "now" in Egypt but not during the conquest of Canaan. Moses had an almost boundless love for God and His people, and the delay in their salvation from bondage made him impatient. This same impatience drove him to embrace the rabble who sought conversion and, finally, to strike the rock instead of speaking to it at Mei Merivah (*Numbers* 20:12).

How is not producing male heirs an appropriate retribution for Joshua's sin of inappropriately offering a legal decision?

The Torah in its written form is really no more than brief notes of the vast body of the Oral Law. In fact, without a solid prior knowledge of the Oral Law, we would not understand the Written Law. The Oral Law comes down to us from generation to generation by an unbroken chain of Sages tracing all the way back to Moses. When a student renders decisions prematurely, he in effect steps outside the chain and circumvents its well-ordered linkage; he acts as if a new chain starts with him. God responds measure for measure (*middah keneged middah*), his own personal links are also weakened, and he is left without male heirs. Providence directs that no chain appears to start from him.

vii. *Mitigating Circumstances*

Seeming redundancies in the Torah always signal hidden meaning. Consequently, the account of Miriam's slander against her brother invites notice (12:1). "Miriam and Aaron spoke against Moses regarding the Cushite woman he had married, for he had married a Cushite woman."

Why does the Torah tell us twice in the same breath that Moses married a Cushite woman? Furthermore, why doesn't the Torah identify Zipporah by her proper name?

It would appear that even as the Torah chastises Miriam for her transgression it also presents exculpatory factors in her defense. Miriam disapproved of Moses ceasing to have conjugal relations with Zipporah. She felt it was inappropriate asceticism even for a prophet, and she raised the subject with Aaron. This conversation had a slanderous hue, and God afflicted Miriam with the skin lesions of *tzaraas*.

Earlier in the *parashah*, the Torah records (10:29-32) that Moses attempted to dissuade his father-in-law Jethro from leaving. The implication is that he didn't succeed. According to one Midrash, Jethro left and later returned. In any case, at the time of the fateful conversation between Miriam and Aaron, Jethro was gone. Consequently, Zipporah no longer had the support of a father living nearby, and Miriam sprang to her defense when she heard that her brother was no longer fulfilling his conjugal obligations.

The Torah repeatedly identifies Zipporah as a Cushite woman to draw our attention to her situation. She was a convert from an alien people without relatives or anyone else to champion her cause. Miriam sinned in slandering Moses, but she was not without virtuous motivation; there were mitigating circumstances.

viii. *Miriam's Timing*

OVER A YEAR HAD PASSED FROM THE TIME MOSES SEPARATED from his wife until Miriam and Aaron, his siblings, slandered him for it. Why did they suddenly decide to take him to task for old history? The Midrash (*Tanchuma; Sifrei* 99) explains that when Zipporah heard Eldad and Meidad prophesying in the camp, she remarked that it seemed their wives would soon lose their conjugal companionship. Miriam understood the implication's of her sister-in-law's remark, although she had no prior inkling of it, and she immediately raised the subject with Aaron.

Another explanation can be offered based on the frenetic pace of events during that year. The Jewish people received the Torah in the beginning of Sivan. For the next one hundred and twenty days, Moses was on Mount Sinai and obviously unavailable to his wife. When he returned on Yom Kippur, a light emanated from his face (*Exodus* 34:35), and the Divine Presence dwelled in his tent, where the Tablets of the Ten Commandments were stored; under these circumstances, Moses could not be with his wife. This situation persisted until the *Mishkan* was erected on the first of Nissan in the second year.

Once Moses erected the *Mishkan,* he devoted twelve days to its inauguration as the dwelling place of the Divine Presence. For the next thirty-eight days, until the Jewish people left Sinai on the twentieth of the second month of the second year, Moses was preoccupied with teaching numerous laws regarding the Divine service and the imminent conquest of the land. The needs of the community preempted his own personal obligations for the time being.

Things did not get much better once the journey began. At the first stop, in Kivros HaTaavah, Moses had his hands full with two quasi-rebellions. But the second way station, a place called Chatzeros (whose name recalls a dwelling place), presented no such problems. The people were prepared, on the verge of entering the land. The atmosphere was tranquil. There were no uprisings, no crises. And still, Moses remained separated from his wife.

Miriam now understood that Moses had ceased having conjugal relations with his wife because of his role as prophet, and she complained to Aaron about his behavior. The Jewish people would soon be entering the land, and the miraculous conduct of their affairs would come to an end. In the long run, the achievement of perfection in human life lies in the elevation of the mundane. The ideal Jewish man, modeled after the Kohen Gadol, must be married. Judaism does not espouse a monkish life. Rather, it finds the potential for elevation and holiness in the physical as well. With the Jewish people on the threshold of the Holy Land, there was no longer, in Miriam's opinion, any justification for Moses' celibacy.

But Miriam erred. She did not factor in the singular nature of Moses' prophecy. It was a level of connection to God that would not tolerate this aspect of earthly existence.

ix. *Aaron's Painful Punishment*

MIRIAM AND AARON BOTH SLANDERED MOSES, YET GOD afflicted only Miriam (12:1,9-10). "Miriam and Aaron spoke against Moses regarding the Cushite woman he had married . . . the wrath of God burned up against them . . . and behold, Miriam was afflicted with *tzaraas* like snow, and Aaron turned to Miriam, and behold, she was afflicted with *tzaraas*." Although Aaron also participated in the slanderous talk, there is no mention of God punishing him. Why did God exempt him from punishment?

The *Sifrei* (12:1) notes a grammatical incongruity in the verse. The verb for "[they] spoke" appears in the singular feminine form (וַתְּדַבֵּר) even though both Miriam and Aaron are the subjects. Apparently, Miriam initiated the slanderous exchange and bore the primary responsibility.

This explains why God afflicted only Miriam with *tzaraas*, the ultimate supernatural manifestation of *lashon hara*. It still leaves unexplained why Aaron escaped with no punishment whatsoever. He also spoke, albeit after Miriam did. Moreover, he certainly listened to her speak. Surely, he bore some responsibility, since slander requires both a speaker and a listener; in fact, our Sages consider the listener, who abets the crime, more sinful than the speaker. According to this, Aaron deserved even greater punishment. Where was it?

Actually, Aaron did suffer a painful punishment, and we find it right here in the verse. Aaron's overriding characteristic was his immeasurable love for his fellow man. Just seeing his beloved sister Miriam suffer the affliction of *tzaraas* must have caused him incredible pain.

The *Sifrei* points out a seeming redundancy in the verse, "And behold, Miriam was afflicted with *tzaraas* like snow, and Aaron turned to Miriam, and behold, she was afflicted with *tzaraas*." What do we learn from the second mention of her *tzaraas*? The *Sifrei* states that Miriam's *tzaraas* broke out anew whenever Aaron looked at her. Here we see the sharp edges of Aaron's punishment. Every time he looked at his sister he was made excruciatingly aware of his role in her distress. This was a horrible punishment indeed for a man of utmost love and kindness.

Aaron's desperate plea to Moses to cure Miriam, and his admission of guilt, reflect his suffering (12:11), "I beg you, my lord, do not cast a sin upon us, for we have been foolish and we have sinned."

x. *Therapeutic Illness*

HAPHAZARD ILLNESS DOES NOT APPEAR IN THE TORAH. When Miriam falls ill with *tzaraas*, it is in retribution for her slander, and Moses responds with prayer (12:13), "And Moses cried to God saying, 'Please, O Lord, please heal her.' " He seeks no medical attention for her.

Secular humanist society sees illness as an unmitigated evil. In contrast, Judaism views it as an opportunity, a springboard for spiritual growth and increased closeness to God; illness may be spiritually therapeutic. The Talmud (*Berachos* 5a) states that a person should respond to illness by examining his behavior for signs of sin. Although physicians are given permission to heal (*Exodus* 21:19; *Bava Kamma* 85a), illness may signal an underlying spiritual malaise requiring correction. According to the Ramban, a person on a high spiritual level should spurn medical attention and rely on God to effect his recovery. Along these lines, the Talmud (*Pesachim* 56a) praises King Hezekiah for destroying the esoteric Book of Remedies; illness should be a catalyst to self-examination and improvement, prodding a person to intensify his relationship with God. By seeking medical attention and a humanly effected cure, a person forfeits this opportunity.

In the daily *Shemoneh Esrei,* in the special prayer for the sick, we say, "Heal us, O God, and we will be healed. Save us and we will be saved. For You are our praise. Give rise to a complete healing to all our wounds, for You are Lord, King, faithful and compassionate Healer. Blessed are You, O God, Healer of the sick of His people Israel."

In the central set of thirteen blessings that ask for the fulfillment of our needs, we describe God as King in only four prayers — for repentance, forgiveness, healing and justice. This impresses on us that our illnesses frequently derive from our insubordination to God as King, from our failure before the bar of justice. And in all cases, illness is within His regal and just decree. Illness is not a random occurrence, an impersonal malfunction of nature we ask God to repair. It is a sign of spiritual opportunity; physical healing may flow from our spiritual ascent.

By referring to God as the Creator of Cure (*Borei Refuos*), our prayers underscore the concept that all healing is under a special province. When the term *borei* is used for creation it indicates the creation of something from nothing, *creatio ex nihilo*. Healing involves more than a knowledge and manipulation of physical properties. God's will is uniquely present, just as it is present in our sickness.

פרשת שלח
Parashas Shelach

i. Messengers Gone Astray

LONG BEFORE THE SPIES SET OUT ON THEIR ILL-FATED MISsion, Moses already suspected something would go wrong (13:16). "These are the names of the men Moses sent to reconnoiter the land. And Moses called Hosea, son of Nun, Joshua." Why did he change Hosea's name to Joshua? Our Sages (*Tanchuma* 6, *Sotah* 34b) tells us that the new name means "God save." Moses prayed that God would save Joshua from the conspiracy of the spies. Why was Moses suspicious? Why did he feel this particular intervention was necessary? And why did he single out Joshua from among the twelve spies for special consideration?

The Talmud (*Berachos* 34b) notes, "A messenger's failure reflects badly on his sender." This aphorism displays a sensitivity to the subtleties of human nature. A messenger's dedication and enthusiasm usually reflect his perception of the sender's attitude. If he believes the sender cares deeply, he will extend himself to be successful; the messenger, having accepted the sender's mission, will do his best to satisfy him. But if the messenger deems the sender indifferent or negative to the mission, he himself will take a cavalier attitude toward its successful fulfillment. For instance, a pious rabbi and an indifferent Jew both send the same messenger to purchase a *lulav*, the palm branch used for the Succos ritual, offering no additional instructions. The messenger will undoubtedly purchase a first-rate *lulav* for the rabbi and an acceptable one for the indifferent Jew. Although nothing is spoken out, the messenger's perception of the sender's preference will determine his actions.

Although God did not forbid the sending of the spies, Deuteronomy makes clear (1:22-23) that He did not approve of it either. Nonetheless, the weaker elements among the Jewish people, insecure in their relationship with God, persisted in their request for a reconnoitering mission before entry to the land; they did not have sufficient faith that God would deliver the land into their hands. Grounded in spiritual deficiency, the mission was doomed to failure from the beginning. Sensing the negativism of the senders, the messengers adjusted the thrust of their mission accordingly.

Moses perceived the reluctance of the senders to enter the land and understood that the mission was destined for catastrophe. The people's desire to send spies gave credence to the prophecy of Eldad and Meidad that Moses would not lead the conquest of the land. In order to protect his beloved protégé from this impending disaster, Moses changed his name to Joshua. This act identified Joshua as specifically Moses' messenger and imbued his role in the overall mission with the passion and enthusiasm of his great sender.

ii. *Instant Forgiveness*

SUCCESSFUL APOLOGIES ELICIT FORGIVENESS IN THE FUTURE tense ("I will forgive you") or the present ("I forgive you") tense. Yet when Moses pleads with God to forgive the Jewish people following the incident of the spies, He responds in the past tense (14:20), "And God said, '*Salachti*. I forgave you.' "

The syntax of God's forgiveness underscores that which we already know. No passage of time separates God's will from His actions. Particularly with regard to the Jewish people's repentance, the Torah emphasizes that the instant God accepted Moses' prayer the forgiveness had already been granted.

iii. Just Short of Forty

BEFORE THE INCIDENT OF THE SPIES, THE JEWISH PEOPLE were a three-day march from Canaan, on the cusp of conquest. Tragically, the spies' slander delayed their entry for nearly four decades (14:34). "You shall bear your iniquities by the number of days that you spied out the land, forty days, a day for a year, a day for a year, forty years."

The Jewish people spent a total of forty years in the inhospitable desert. God issued the decree barring them from the land on the ninth of Av (the fifth month) in the second year, which means that God extended their stay in the desert by just under thirty-nine years. Why does the Torah call it forty years?

We may easily explain this discrepancy if the reference to forty years is to the total number of years in the desert. Still, why would the retribution of the forty-day mission encompass the elapsed time as well? One could argue that there really is no direct year by year relationship, rather it is a more general correlation of a unit of forty to a unit of forty. The simple meaning of the verse, however, seems to make a correlation between each individual day to an additional individual year in the desert. How can this be if the numbers do not match?

We find similar language with regard to court-administered lashes (*Deuteronomy* 25:2-3). "It shall be that if the wicked one deserves lashes, the judge shall cast him down and strike him before him, according to his wickedness, by a count. Forty shall he strike him, he shall add no more."

Our Sages determined (*Makkos* 22a) that the actual count of lashes is only thirty-nine lashes. They read the words *b'mispar arba'im*, "by a count of forty," as "a count that approximates forty," meaning thirty-nine. The Torah uses similar language here, *b'mispar yamin . . . arba'im*, "by a count of forty days," which would be interpreted as "a count that approximates forty days." Just as the Torah mercifully reduced the number of lashes administered to a transgressor by one, so did God mercifully reduce the exile of the Jewish people in the desert by one year, from forty to thirty-nine. Just as the transgressor removes his wicked label through stripes, so too, after thirty-nine years, God considered the Jewish people cleansed.

iv. *The Late Warriors*

WITH THE DOOR TO THE HOLY LAND SLAMMED IN THEIR faces as a result of the spies' slander, the faint-hearted people suddenly found new reservoirs of courage, but it was too late (14:44-45). "[Despite Moses' prediction of failure,] they defiantly ascended to the mountaintop . . . The Amalekite and the Canaanite who dwelt on the mountain descended; they struck and pounded them until Charmah."

The word that portrays their defiant attack on the mountain, *vayapilu* (וַיַּעְפִּלוּ), appears nowhere else in the Torah. The commentators seek hidden meanings that would justify the use of this unusual word. Ibn Ezra discerns an allusion to clouds, which suggests that fear or guilt motivated them to act in stealth. *Targum Yonasan,* relying on the interchangeability of the similar-sounding *aleph* and *ayin*, finds a hint of darkness (*ofel,* אֹפֶל). Here again, the implication is that darkness veiled their fear or guilt.

Perhaps the interchangeable *aleph* and *ayin* reveals yet another nuance of interpretation. The Talmud (Taanis 6b) states that late rains are called *afilah* (אֲפִילָה). Accordingly, the word *vayapilu* suggests that those would-be warriors who ventured forth under cover of clouds or darkness were a day too late (and thirty-nine years too early).

v. The Wood Gatherer

IT WAS A TRAGIC TIME. THE JEWISH PEOPLE WERE ON THE verge of entering the Promised Land, but the disastrous chain of events beginning with the slanderous spies ruined everything. God decreed that the people would remain in the desert for a total of forty years, until the entire generation died and another took its place.

In the immediate aftermath, a strange incident takes place (15:32-35), "The people of Israel were in the desert, and they found a man gathering wood on the Sabbath. Those who found him gathering wood brought him to Moses, Aaron and the entire assembly. They placed him in detention, for it had not been clarified what should be done to him. And God said to Moses, 'The man shall be put to death; the entire assembly shall pelt him with stones outside the camp.' "

How does this episode connect to the preceding incident of

the spies? Furthermore, what is the purpose of the seemingly superfluous information that the people of Israel were "in the desert (*bamidbar*)"?

The expression "they found a man gathering wood" is also puzzling. Ordinarily, the Torah would state that "there was a man gathering wood." The words "they found" implies that people were looking. What does this mean? The *Sifrei* explains that Moses posted sentries to watch for any violations of the Sabbath. If so, a new question arises. Why did Moses choose to investigate the nation's Sabbath observance at this point?

Moses understood that the Jewish people's eagerness to send spies and readiness to accept their slanderous report reflected a collective failure of trust in God's providence. Opposed to this, Sabbath observance reinforces and gives testimony to God's general providence over mankind and His particular providence over the Jewish people; the Torah describes the Sabbath as a remembrance of the Creation and the Exodus. Presumably, Moses suspected that the collective deficiency in trust would manifest itself in a lax attitude toward Sabbath observance. Therefore, he posted sentries to warn against transgression and apprehend any violators. By raising the general level of Sabbath observance in the aftermath of the spies, Moses addressed their deficiencies and reinforced their collective trust in God.

Now let us consider for a moment. What did the wood gatherer intend to do with the wood? Rashi, in his commentary on the Talmud (*Beitzah* 33b), states that the primary use of wood is for construction. Let us then assume the wood gatherer intended to build a wooden house. Ever since entering the desert over a year earlier, the Jewish people had lived in tents. Faced with forty years in the desert, however, a wooden house beckoned as a more secure and comfortable abode than a tent. Thus, the wood gatherer sought security, because he lacked sufficient trust in God, the very flaw that had caused the disaster of the spies. The Torah emphasizes this last point with the gratuitous statement that they were "in the desert (*bamidbar*)."

After the return of the spies, the word *midbar* occurs ten times in the *parashah*, corresponding to the number of spies who slandered the land. The mention of *midbar* again here in connection with the wood gatherer associates the two events. The desecration of the Sabbath echoes the underlying flaw that led to the debacle of the spies.

There is some disagreement among the commentators as to the chronology of events. Some follow the simple meaning of the verse and place the episode of the wood gatherer immediately after the incident of the spies. Rashi, quoting the *Mechilta,* states that it took place a year earlier, shortly after the Exodus. Even so, the same explanation holds true, for the Torah places these two events side by side. In both cases, insufficient trust was the root cause of the sin.

Right after the episode of the wood gatherer, the Torah commands the placement of *tzitzis*, fringes, at the corners of one's garment (15:40-41) "in order that you remember to perform all the commandments and be holy for the Lord. I am God, your Lord, who brought you forth from the land of Egypt to be a Lord to you, I am God, your Lord."

Clothing are a person's most immediate physical protection, and the *tzitzis* attached to them continually remind the wearer that God provides his true protection. The Jewish people had forgotten this important truth, and this led to the spies and the wood gatherer. The *tzitzis* would serve as a constant reminder and would hopefully prevent recurrences in the future.

Between the incident of the spies and the episode of the wood gatherer, the Torah presents several commandments. The first, which concerns oaths, begins with the phrase "when you will enter the land." The second, which concerns tithes, also mentions that "I will bring you into the land." These serve as reassurance to the people that although they sinned and were barred from the land, their children would eventually enter and take possession of it.

The final commandments concern the communal and individual obligation to seek atonement for the sin of idolatry. These, too, offered reassurance to the Jewish people. They had come to the brink of destruction; only Moses' intervention had saved them. Now they faced forty years in the desert, and they could easily have surrendered to despair. What assurances were there that another sin would not result in complete annihilation? By showing them the possibility of repentance, God indicated that He would give the Jewish people a method to remain close to Him no matter how severe the sin, even to the extent of idolatry, provided they were earnest in their desire to return to Him.

vi. *Foregone Conclusions*

WHAT DO SPIES HAVE TO DO WITH FRINGED GARMENTS? Apparently, a lot. The Torah presents the commandment of *tzitzis* with an unusual word (15:39). "It shall be *tzitzis* for you that you may see it and remember all God's commandments and perform them; do not be distracted (*lo sasuru*) by your heart and your eyes, after which you stray." The word *sasuru* is strongly reminiscent of the tragic incident of the spies (13:1-2). "And God spoke to Moses, saying, 'Send forth men if you please and let them scout (*veyasuru*) the land.' " The words *sasuru* and *veyasuru* both derive from the root verb *lasur*, to scout.

The Talmud (*Sanhedrin* 104b) observes that the prophet Jeremiah arranged the verses of the Book of Lamentations in the alphabetical order of their first letters. In both the third and fourth chapters, however, a single anomaly appears. The verse beginning with the letter *peh* precedes the verse beginning with *ayin*, even though *ayin* follows *peh* in the alphabet. The Talmud explains that Jeremiah alluded to the ancient historical cause of the nation's cataclysm. The word *peh* also means mouth, while the word *ayin* also means eye. By putting the *peh* before the *ayin*, Jeremiah referred to the spies, who lived a thousand years earlier, and spoke before seeing. By going off to scout the land with an intent to find fault, they planted the seeds of disaster.

The meaning of the word *lasur*, therefore, is to look with the expectation of confirming foregone conclusions. The more common word for looking, *lir'os*, means looking with an open mind. This distinction between two types of looking is delineated in the commandment of *tzitzis*, where *lir'os* applies to the *tzitzis* while *lasur* applies to following the whims of the heart.

A close reading of the *Haftarah* further validates this distinction. When it tells the story of the spies Joshua sent to Jericho, no forms of the verb *lasur* appear in the narrative, only forms of the verb *lir'os*.[1] They reported what they saw, not what they wanted or expected to see. And what did they see? A populace terrified by the approach of the Jewish people. After forty years, the memories of the spectacular defeat of the Egyptian armies must have faded somewhat, and yet, the populace remained terrified.

Surely, they were no less terrified when the original spies came to scout the land. Why didn't they see it? Because they had already reached their conclusion beforehand; they had closed their minds.

The commandment of *tzitzis* addresses this human failing — the tendency to rationalize to satisfy emotional needs, to see what we want to see. By letting the Torah guide us, God graces us with the objectivity and stability that enable us to avoid the pitfalls of temptation.

---

1. Although Moses himself did command the spies to "scout the land," using the word *lasur*, he undoubtedly meant them to go with positive foregone conclusions, based not on their emotions but on God's assurance that the land was good.

vii. Untangled Fringes

THE FRINGES ON OUR GARMENTS ARE UBIQUITOUS reminders (15:39), "It shall be *tzitzis* for you that you may see it and remember all God's commandments and perform them." How do the *tzitzis* remind us of the commandments? One explanation the Rabbis offer is that the numerical value of the word *tzitzis* is 600. In addition, each fringe has 8 strings and 5 knots, for a total of 613, the number of commandments in the Torah.

The *Shulchan Aruch* mandates that we examine our fringes daily for torn or missing strings, which would invalidate the fulfillment of the commandment. The *Mishnah Berurah,* quoting from the Midrash, points out that the word *tzitzis* is an acronym for the phrase "a righteous person always untangles the strands of his *tzitzis* (צַדִּיק יְפָרֵשׁ צִיצִית תָּמִיד - ציצת)." Beyond the basic benefit of insuring that none of the strands have broken, to what additional piety does the Midrash allude in the extra measure of untangling the strands?

Perhaps an analogy would best illustrate the intent. A meal of meat, mashed potatoes and mixed vegetables is served. A rough-mannered fellow might stab a piece of meat with his fork, dunk it into the potatoes, sweep up some mixed vegetables and shove the entire hodgepodge into his mouth. A person of more refined tastes, however, will eat each item separately to savor its individual flavors. The same applies to the performance of the mitzvos. Some people may be inclined to group them all together as generic tasks that need to be done, and often the quicker the better. But those who have a finer appreciation for the commandments will perform each one slowly, carefully and individually to extract and absorb all the spiritual flavors it contains.

The *tzitzis* represent the commandments of the Torah, and the righteous untangle the strands. They strive to gain the full benefit and joy of each and every one as a vehicle for achieving an ever closer relationship with God.

The Torah requires that one strand at each corner of the *tzitzis* be *techeiles*, an aquamarine-dyed wool. Our Sages observe that *techeiles* is cognate with *tachlis*, purpose. This is the function of the *tzitzis*, to remind us of our purpose, that we are here to fulfill God's commandments.

The Jerusalem Talmud (*Berachos* 1:2) explains that the color of *techeiles* is reminiscent of the sea, which is reminiscent of the sky, which is reminiscent of God's Throne of Glory. We see that *techeiles* is the color of the horizon, where earth and sea meet the sky; the dyed strand serves as a symbolic reminder of our purpose on this earth, to create in the physical realm a place where God's presence is manifest, where heaven meets earth.

The Midrash (*Bereishis Rabbah, Vayeitzei*) reports that the *techeiles* dye was manufactured in the city of Luz. In the Book of Genesis (28:9), we learned that Luz was the ancient name of the site where Jacob dreamed of the descending and ascending angels on a celestial ladder, the future site of the Temple. We explained that the word *luz* reflects the idea of a ladder connecting heaven and earth: the intellectual or spiritual connecting to the earthly forces in man. Fittingly, the color *techeiles*, which represents the same merging, was made in a city called Luz.

viii. *Attach a Red Ribbon*

THE *HAFTARAH* RELATES THE STORY OF THE SPIES JOSHUA sent to Jericho before the Jewish people invaded and conquered Canaan. Rachav, a Canaanite harlot, helped the spies avert capture by diverting the police. She told them that the Jewish intruders had set off in a different direction from the one they had planned to take. In return, she asked that she and her family be spared when the Jews stormed Jericho. The spies agreed and told her to attach a red ribbon to her house as a protective signal to the invaders.

Rachav followed their instructions (*Joshua* 2:21), "[The spies] went out, and she attached the red ribbon to her window." Her timing, however, seems strange. Apparently, even with the invasion still weeks away, Rachav tied the red ribbon to her window as soon as the spies left. Why would she do so? Since it was already known in Jericho that Rachav had met the spies, wouldn't a red ribbon on her window arouse suspicion?

Rachav's clever ruse revealed her keen grasp of human psychology. By waiting until just before the attack, she would run the risk of people remembering that the spies had visited her and putting two and two together. She might be arrested and executed. Even if not, perhaps others would copy her and tie red ribbons to their own windows and thereby violate the terms of her agreement with the spies — at the cost of her own life. On the other hand, if she attached the ribbon immediately, long before the Jewish attack seemed imminent, people would not suspect it might be a sign. Later, in the heat of the battle, they would not suspect that the red ribbon placed there weeks earlier was the sign of a safe house.

פרשת קרח
Parashas Korach

i. What Moses Heard

ON MORE THAN ONE OCCASION, THE JEWISH PEOPLE BELEAguered Moses in the desert, complaining vociferously about the lack of water and meat among other privations. Korach, however, was the first to challenge Moses' authority directly. Moses reacted in an unusual manner (16:4), "And Moses heard and fell on his face." What is the meaning of this reaction? What did he "hear"? Why did he "fall on his face"?

At first glance, the words "and Moses heard" are superfluous. Of course, he heard. After all, they were speaking to him. In earlier episodes of malcontents complaining to Moses, the Torah never tells us that "he heard"; why does the Torah do so here? According to several Midrashic sources, (*Sanhedrin* 110a, *Targum Yonasan, Tanchuma* 10, *Midrash Rabbah* 18), the Torah implies that Korach slandered Moses with charges of adultery. Other sources and commentators, however, take the words at face value. If so, what did he "hear"?

Perhaps the most common cause of rift and rebellion is the

feeling of being ignored and disenfranchised, the feeling that no one is listening. In fact, conflicts can very often be resolved by the simple act of attentive listening, even when no solutions are offered. People will tolerate partial or inadequate solutions, or even no solutions at all, as long as they and their complaints are validated, as long as they feel their concerns are being taken into account. Revolutionary wars have been fought because people felt they were denied "representation."

When Moses saw the people were in revolt, his first response was to listen carefully to the complaints of Korach and his followers. He showed them that "he heard," that he understood their frustration. Regardless of the relative merits of Korach's complaint, Moses conveyed importance to Korach by listening attentively.

Then Moses "fell on his face" in response to Korach's criticism (16:3) that Moses had "exalted himself excessively above the congregation." The *Ohr HaChaim* explains that by falling on his face Moses expressed humility rather than fear. Had Moses really been driven by a desire for self-aggrandizement, even in a small way, he surely would have responded with arrogant anger. By his humble response, Moses demonstrated that personal ambition was not a part of his motivation. Although Moses failed to quell peacefully the only revolt that directly challenged his role as God's chosen leader, he demonstrated to all future generations the hallmarks of leadership in the face of dissension and rebellion.

ii. Recombinant Etymology

THE BOOK OF CREATION (*SEFER HAYETZIRAH*) STATES, "[Before the world was created,] God carved out the thirty-two paths of wisdom." These are the twenty-two letters of the Hebrew alphabet and the ten cardinal numbers; these are the channels through which the infinite wisdom of the Creator flows into the world.

Many ideas and concepts are associated with the forms and meanings of the individual letters. For instance, the letters *dalet* (ד) and *reish* (ר) are similar in appearance, being open on the left side, and the words they represent, *rash* and *dal*, both refer to a needy person. But there is a difference. A *dal* is needy in the sense that he yearns for greater spirituality, while a *rash* strives for material things.

Our Sages point out that the letters *hei* (ה) and *kuf* (ק), which are next to the *dalet* and *reish* respectively, are both constructed by inserting a letter into the left-side opening of the *dalet or reish*. Inserting a *yud* (י) forms the *hei*; both the *hei* and the *yud* form God's Name and are associated with spirituality.[1] The insertion transforms the spiritual *dal* into the spiritual *hei*. Conversely, the letter *kuf* means monkey, a creature that mimics the physicality of humans but not their intellect and spirituality. It is formed by inserting the letter *zayin* (ז) into the open end of the *reish*. The letter *zayin* is associated with man's appetitive, sexual and aggressive nature, his most animalistic aspects. Thus, when the materially deprived *rash* connects with his animalistic drives, he become a monkey, a caricature of a human being.

Now let us observe what occurs when the *reish* and the *dalet* are combined with the letter *ayin* (ע), which means eye. The *ayin*, which has a numerical value of 70, is associated with investigation and gathering of information, correlating with the 70 sages who comprise the Sanhedrin, the high court. When an *ayin* is placed after a *dalet*, it forms the word *da* (דַע), which means knowledge; the spiritual seeker who investigates discovers knowledge. When it is placed after a *reish*, however, it forms the word *ra* (רַע), which means evil or unstable; the seeker of pleasures finds evil.

---

1. The Talmud (*Menachos* 29b) states that God created the universe with the letter *hei* and the spiritual universe with the letter *yod*.

Moses derides Korach's followers as "wicked men" (16:26). The word used here for the wicked is *rasha* (רָשָׁע), which combines *reish* and *ayin* and also adds a *shin* (שׁ), which connotes material abundance and completeness. The *rasha* pursues (*ayin*) and fills (*shin*) his material greed (*reish*).

iii. *Vanished Without a Trace*

FACED WITH KORACH'S REBELLION, MOSES DECLARES TO the Jewish people (16:28-30), "With this you shall know that God has sent me to perform all these deeds, that it was not my own idea, if [Korach and his followers] die as all men do, if they meet the fate of all men, then God did not send me. But if God forms a new creation and the earth opens its mouth and swallows them and all they possess, and they go down living to the netherworld, then you shall know that these men infuriated God."

Why did Moses make his vindication dependent on Korach dying a bizarre death? Why couldn't he say simply that if Korach dies a sudden death, it is proof positive that he, Moses, is the rightful leader? Why was there a need for a "new creation"? Furthermore, why was it necessary for the earth to swallow all of Korach's possessions?

Moses wanted to demonstrate that challenges to the Torah and distortions of its concepts have no place in this world. God would obliterate Korach and his heretical view of Torah until not even the slightest vestige of anything connected with him or his identity remained in existence.

The theme that there is no place in creation for those who seek to thwart God's will appears frequently in the Torah. God commands us to obliterate all traces of Amalek, to blot out their remembrance. Likewise, God commands that we incinerate – lock, stock and barrel – a city whose inhabitants have all practiced idolatry. When the Egyptians refused to let the Jewish people travel three days into the desert to worship God, He afflicted them with three days of a palpable darkness that immobilized them completely. The message was clear. Those who would block God's mission for the Jewish people might just as well not exist.

פרשת חקת
Parashas Chukas

i. *The Total Picture*

CONTRADICTION AND MYSTERY CHARACTERIZE THE LAWS of the *parah adumah*, the red heifer (19:2), "This is the decree (*chukas*) of the Torah which God has commanded saying, 'Speak to the people of Israel that they take for you a completely red heifer . . .' " The Torah commands that we burn the red heifer and use its ashes to purify the ritually impure who have come into contact with corpses. Paradoxically, ritually pure people who touch the ashes become impure.

As quoted by Rashi, the Midrash (*Tanchuma* 7) states, "The nations taunt Israel, saying 'What is this point of this commandment?' Therefore, it is written as a *chok*, a Divine decree. You may not question it." Although the Midrash discusses the *parah adumah*, Rashi (*Leviticus* 18:4; *Yoma* 67b) explains that the concept of *chok* applies to all decrees that invite derision or internal doubt. Typical examples are the prohibition against eating the flesh of the swine and the prohibition against wearing *shaatnez*, garments of wool and linen combined.

Apparently, according to the Midrash, *chok* decrees may invite the ridicule of the nations. Yet we find a totally different perspective in the Torah itself (*Deuteronomy* 4:5-8), "Behold, I have taught you decrees and laws, as God, my Lord, has commanded me, which you are to do within the land you are approaching to take possession of it. And you shall safeguard and perform them, for this is your wisdom and insight in the eyes of the peoples that shall hear all these decrees, who shall say, 'This great nation is surely a wise and insightful people!' For which is a great nation that has a God Who is close to it, as is God, our Lord, whenever we call out to Him? And which is a great nation that has righteous decrees (*chukim*) and laws, as this entire Torah that I place before you this day?" Here, the Torah states clearly that the nations will marvel at the wisdom and insight of our "righteous decrees (*chukim*) and laws." How do we resolve this contradiction?

The answer may lie in the phrase "in the eyes of the peoples that shall hear all these decrees," the emphasis being on "all," on seeing the decrees in the context of the Torah's totality. An outsider who focuses on an individual law, such as the prohibition against *shaatnez*, may find it arcane and absurd. If, however, he considers the entire scope of the Torah, with its integrated system of individual and community life that transcends the material world and engenders social harmony and a close relationship with God, he would find its wisdom and insight compelling.

The encounter between Pharaoh and Joseph provides an indication that the qualities of wisdom and insight only emerge when an approach is all encompassing. After Joseph interprets Pharaoh's dreams without hesitation, Joseph offers an unsolicited comprehensive solution to the problems Pharaoh's dreams foretold. Pharaoh responds by immediately selecting Joseph for the job, stating (*Genesis* 41:39), "There is no wise and insightful man like you." Pharaoh uses the exact same words — *chacham v'navon* — Moses does to describe the Jewish people who follow all the Torah's precepts.

These resonant words connect these two passages and bring two thoughts to mind. Pharaoh did not consider Joseph wise and insightful because of his observance of the Torah's statutes. Even today, when so many Jews have unfortunately lost their ties to their ancient moorings, they are still considered wise and insightful people. This manifest characteristic may trace back to our cultural inheritance from Abraham to be seekers of total truth.

Furthermore, Jewish observance in its totality offers us the perfect path to internal and external harmony. A partial measure of the Torah's success in its effects upon us is reflected in the observant community's significantly lower rates of divorce, crime, drugs, school dropouts and other social ills. Historically, it has also been true that other nations and cultures have found the vibrant Jewish community life attractive. Clearly, the observance of the Torah's laws in their totality (*kol,* כָּל) makes us wise and insightful.

Although the Midrash states that we have no right to question the decrees (*chukim*) or search for their rationale, many commentators, Rashi included, do offer various explanations for them. How do we explain this?

Apparently, we must draw a distinction between ascertaining God's ultimate purpose in issuing the decrees and reaping benefits from their study. It is impossible to penetrate the infinite and inscrutable Divine wisdom behind His decrees, just as it is impossible to know God Who is one with His knowledge. We are obliged to desist from such speculation in humble recognition of our limitations as finite creatures. Nonetheless, we may derive profound concepts and insights from the study of these decrees, and we may ascertain some of the benefits in the observance of God's law. These are what the commentators seek to discover.

In this light, we can perhaps discern another teaching in the seemingly contradictory law that the *parah adumah* purifies the impure and contaminates the pure. The contradiction of this law mirrors the paradox of the relationship between our physical and spiritual sides; its very perplexity challenges our tendency to see the physical as the final reality.

ii. Sterile as a Mule

PEOPLE WHO FIND THEMSELVES INDOORS WITH A CORPSE become ritually impure (19:14), "This is the teaching: should a man die in a tent, everything that comes into the tent or is in the tent shall be ritually impure for seven days." The Talmud (*Yevamos* 61a) differentiates between Jewish and non-Jewish corpses, based on the verse's reference to "a man" by the relatively infrequent term *adam* instead of the more common term *ish*. The term *adam* refers exclusively to Jewish people. Gentile corpses, therefore, do not contaminate people under the same roof.

Why does *adam*, which is derived from Adam, refer only to Jewish people? Why doesn't his name encompass all his descendants, including the vast majority of mankind who are non-Jews?

The Talmud (*Yevamos* 98a) states that a convert is not legally considered the son of his non-Jewish father. The source for this rule is Ezekiel, which says of the Egyptians (23:20), "Their flesh is donkey flesh, their issue is the issue of horses."

This verse presents a mixed metaphor, comparing the non-Jewish Egyptian to both a donkey and a horse. What does the prophet convey by combining the metaphors?

Donkeys and horses form a unique animal pair. It may be the only mixed-species union in nature that produces offspring, but that offspring is sterile — the mule. The flesh of the non-Jewish Egyptians may appear to be donkey flesh, but its source is really a horse. Thus, they are actually like sterile mules unable to reproduce. The mixed metaphor is a figurative reference to the empty and alien ideologies of other peoples, which are morally and intellectually bankrupt, sterile after a fashion. They should have inherited the true knowledge of God as an inheritance from their ancestor Adam, but they squandered it. Therefore, they lost their right to be associated with his name, and in death they manifest less impurity.

iii. *The Way Paver*

FINALLY, IN THEIR FORTIETH YEAR IN THE DESERT, THE Jewish people were poised to enter the Holy Land. It should have been a time of transcendent joy, but apparently, it wasn't (21:4-5). "And they journeyed from Mount Hor by way of the Sea of Reeds to bypass the land of Edom, and the people grew irritable along the way. And the people spoke against God and Moses, 'Why did you bring us up from Egypt to die in this desert, for there is no bread and no water, and we are disgusted with the flimsy bread (manna)?' "

Let us consider for a moment the background of these events. These were the children of the emancipated slaves, who had perished in the desert (20:1; see *Rashi*). They had grown up in the most exalted, spiritually focused community that ever existed. They were never concerned with shelter, clothing or food, for God provided all these things miraculously. Under the tutelage of Moses they studied Torah unceasingly and integrated it into their lives. Our Sages considered them the *dor dei'ah*, the generation of knowledge. Could one conceive of a better life? Why would the people "grow irritable"? Why would they speak against God and Moses? Why complain now about manna, which had been satisfactory for forty years?

Furthermore, they had just vanquished the king of Arad in their first battle in the campaign of conquest (21:1ff). They should have been full of confidence and excited anticipation, not irritable. How can we explain their surliness and inappropriate confrontational words?

The answer to this question may lie in the addition of the phrase "along the way" when it would have been sufficient to state that "the people grew irritable." The word "way" (*derech*), which recalls the travels through the desert, brings to mind the recent death of Aaron, for whom the nation had just mourned for thirty days (20:27-29).

Aaron's great virtue was that he loved peace and pursued peace, and in his merit, clouds of glory accompanied the Jewish people through the desert for thirty-nine years. One of the functions of the clouds was to level and smooth the "way" (*derech*) on which they traveled, just as Aaron smoothed the paths of interaction among people by his advocacy of peace.

After Aaron's passing, the "way" became rougher, emotionally because of the loss of his constructive intervention and calming influence and physically because of the loss of the clouds that had come in his merit. Traveling "along the way" was now literally and figuratively rough; people's capacity for tolerance decreased, nerves frayed, tempers flared.

Emotions are fluid and often spill over into other areas; someone frustrated at work may be excessively short-tempered with family members. The people, suddenly squabbling in the absence of Aaron and the clouds, displaced their anger and launched their complaints at God and Moses.

Another factor may have played a role in the timing of the people's complaints. After nearly forty years of almost angelic existence, the people had just begun the process of returning to natural law (*teva*). Since the Exodus, they had lived like Adam before the sin — fed, clothed and sheltered by Divine intervention. Now they were beginning the transition to living in a completely normal, nonmiraculous society in the land of Israel. Moreover, their victorious battle with Arad stimulated their aggressive instincts.

In that state of mind, as they adjusted once again to being more sentient beings, the heavenly manna no longer had the same appeal for them. They became divisive; their aggressive nature had been stimulated by war after lying somewhat dormant for over thirty-nine years. Aaron was no longer present to soothe their ruffled feathers. Complaints once again emerged.

פרשת בלק
Parashas Balak

Copper, Snakes and Sorcery

DO COPPER, SNAKES AND SORCERY HAVE ANYTHING IN common? It would appear that they do. They all share the same Hebrew root word (*nachash,* נָחָשׁ), and they all appear in close proximity to each other in the Book of Numbers, further suggesting an underlying commonality.

In his coerced prophecy about the Jewish people, Balaam declared (23:23), "The Lord brought them forth from Egypt . . . and there is no sorcery (*nichush*) in Jacob." Earlier, the people had complained about the lack of water and the "flimsy bread," but they had a change of heart after serpents attacked them (21:7-9), "And the people approached Moses and said, 'We sinned by speaking against God and you! Pray to God that He remove the serpent (*nachash*) from us.' . . . And Moses made a serpent (*nachash*) of copper (*nechoshes)* and placed it on a pole, and whenever a serpent bit a man, he would look upon the copper serpent and survive."

What is the connection between these three things? Furthermore, why did Moses choose a copper serpent to effect the nation's repentance?

Let us take a closer look at the word *nachash*, which means serpent. It can be deconstructed into two syllables, *nach* (נָח), to rest, and *chash* (חָשׁ), to move swiftly, an accurate description of the serpent's characteristic of lying still then striking quickly. First, it is *nach*, then it is *chash*.

The word *nachash* first appears in the story of the first sin, when the serpent tempted Eve. Our Sages state that the serpent (*nachash*) represents man's *yetzer hara*, the Satan and the Angel of Death. The Torah describes the serpent as the craftiest of all creatures (*arum*). Just as a serpent lies deceptively still before its quick strike, so does a man's *yetzer hara* overcome his resolve with instant rationalizations that lead him toward corruption and perdition; for example, a recovering alcoholic may delude himself that he will have only one drink. Such is man's nature that in his weakness he can quickly be overcome by his basic drives and desires, which frequently lie deceptively dormant.

Copper (*nechoshes*) is a brilliant metal with a goldlike luster. It is, however, only an ersatz precious metal, "fool's gold."[1] Like the serpent, copper is furtively deceptive. Copper is, therefore, an excellent metallic metaphor for the serpent, which personifies the ultimate hidden deceiver. Serpent and copper were, therefore, the combination of image and material Moses considered most effective for therapeutic purposes. By looking at the copper serpent, the people would realize that their desires for pleasures such as fancy foods, like copper, offer only a chimera of the real good, and that they only lead to unexpected and deleterious consequences, like a crafty snake in the grass.

Sorcery (*nichush*), which fools the unsuspecting victim by sudden trickery, also has this negative quality of deceptiveness.[2] When Balaam cast his malevolent gaze on the Jewish people, however, his prophetic experience did not detect any sorcery

1. In the prophecy of Isaiah (60:17), God promises to replace copper with gold in the Messianic era.

2. There are varying opinions as to what exactly constitutes *nichush*. Nonetheless, regardless of whether it is some form of magic or a metaphysical communication, *nichush* is a deceptive practice forbidden to Jews, who must place their trust in God.

(*nichush*) in Jacob. At that moment, following the repentance inspired by the copper serpent (*nachash hanechoshes*), God had refined the nation like metal in the hands of its smelter. They were pure and had no room for the trickery of sorcery (*nichush)* spawned by the *yetzer hara*.

Such is the nature of the *yetzer hara*. It beguiles man and draws him away from God. Such is the nature of the infinite wisdom of God's language that it reveals the connection between snake, copper and sorcery, and the subterranean passages of the mind and heart through which the *yetzer hara* travels.

פרשת פנחס
Parashas Pinchas

i. The Ultimate Shield

PRUDENCE, GOES THE OLD SAYING, IS THE BETTER PART OF valor. Bravery is a virtue, but only as long as it doesn't overstep the line that separates courage from foolhardiness. Moses quite sensibly asked God that his replacement be a courageous leader, but he also asked that he lead the troops into battle, as would King David centuries later (27:17; *Rashi*). Was this prudent? Would it be wise for a general to risk his life by placing himself in the heat of the battle?

In the annals of warfare, a king or general rarely rides into battle at the head of his armies. A general is simply too valuable an asset to risk. Moreover, a general at the front would be in greater danger than an ordinary officer, because the enemy would throw all its forces directly at him; a decapitated army is an incapacitated army. In the short run, the general's presence might inspire the troops, but in the long run, the loss of a general would cripple the army. Why then would Moses want his replacement to lead the troops into battle?

Unlike the general providence that governs the fortunes of all peoples, the Jewish people exist under a special Divine providence. This is particularly true when the entire nation and its leader are at risk. Enemy troops may launch thick clouds of arrows at the Jewish leader, but none will find its mark if it is not specifically so ordained. When he leads his troops into battle, a Jewish leader underscores the important point that faith in God is the Jewish nation's ultimate shield, that his and the nation's spiritual shortcomings are far more threatening than enemy weapons.

Moses wanted a Jewish leader who would be in the forefront of battle. He wanted a leader who understood that the Jewish people, and their leader in particular, were under an intimate Divine providence. Such an attitude would convey to the Jewish soldiers that only fealty to God and His Torah would bring them victory.

Moses also asked God that his replacement lead the Jewish armies back from battle. What was the purpose of this request? What difference could it possibly make?

There are two outcomes to war — victory and defeat. In victory, it is common for conquering troops to vent their triumphant exhilaration in a rampage of pillage and plunder. A Jewish leader, the moral shepherd of his people, cannot allow this to happen. Once the battle is won, he must lead the troops home sober and humble in the knowledge that it is God who has delivered their enemies into their hands.

Conversely, if the battle should end in defeat, leaders of lesser virtue shift the blame to underlings and downplay their own roles. Not so the ideal Jewish leader. He takes full responsibility for whatever takes place. Even if his troops return home with heads hung in defeat, he stands at the head of his troops, bearing the blame. And he leads the people to self-examination and repentance.

ii. *Falling Through the Cracks*

SPEAR IN HAND, PINCHAS STRODE INTO THE ENCAMPMENT and impaled the Jewish prince Zimri as he coupled with a Midianite princess, stemming the plague that had claimed twenty-four thousand lives. For this, God duly rewarded him (25:10-13). "And God spoke to Moses, saying, 'Pinchas, son of Elazar, son of Aaron the Kohen, deflected My wrath from the people of Israel when he wrought My vengeance among them, so I did not annihilate the people of Israel in My vengeance. Therefore, say, "Behold, I give him My covenant of peace." And it shall be a covenant of eternal priesthood for him and his offspring after him for his having taken vengeance for his Lord and atoned for the people of Israel.' "

The paradox is striking. God rewards Pinchas for his violent, albeit justifiable, act of vengeance with an eternal covenant of peace! God also gives him an eternal covenant of priesthood (Kehunah), which in itself includes the priestly blessing to the people: "May God grant you peace." How do we reconcile Pinchas' reward of peace with his ferocious and violent vengeance on God's behalf?

Our Sages (*Avos* 1:12) praise Pinchas' righteous grandfather Aaron, the patriarch of the priesthood, for "loving God's creatures" (*oheiv es habrios*). Love of his fellow man was one of Aaron's overriding virtues, and yet it still required balance.

Twice in the Torah do we find Aaron liable to punishment. The first is when Aaron participated passively in the construction of the Golden Calf in order to stall for time. In Deuteronomy (9:20), Moses reveals that he had successfully intervened to save Aaron from death at that time. The second occasion is at Mei Merivah, where God commands Moses and Aaron to bring forth water from a rock by speaking to it but Moses strikes it instead (20:7ff). As a result, both Moses and Aaron are barred from entry to the Holy Land; they must die in the desert. In this case, only Moses hit the rock, and yet Aaron is guilty for his passive acquiescence to Moses' act. We may find a commonality of these failings. We may suggest that in both instances Aaron's great love of humanity led to a small lack of immediate zeal to criticize and find fault in another human being.

Aaron's principal trait, which was to set the tone for all future Kohanim, was his love for his fellow man. This great virtue, however, carries the risk of imbalance. The Kohanim's love of humanity needed to be balanced with zeal on God's behalf. The word *shalom*, peace, is best translated as harmony. Pinchas' act of zealotry for God balanced the scales for the Kehunah by introducing zeal into the equation. Henceforth, Kohanim were characterized not only by love for man but also by zeal for God; in the Talmud, we find that rabbinic regulations do not apply in the Temple. They are unnecessary, because the priests are *zerizim* (diligent). God rewarded Pinchas with the eternal covenant of priesthood and peace in recognition of the balance he had brought to the Kehunah with his seminal act of zealotry. He brought a true and lasting peace, a harmonious peace.

Why, of all the Kohanim, did only Pinchas see clearly the need to temper love with zeal? The answer may lie in his personal background. Initially, Pinchas had actually been excluded from the priesthood. When God initiated Aaron and his sons Elazar and Isamar into the priesthood (*Leviticus* 8:1ff), Elazar's son Pinchas was too young to be invested in his own right. But since he had already been born at the time of the investiture, he could not claim hereditary sanctity as would his brothers and their future descendants. In effect, Pinchas was excluded from the priesthood. He had fallen through the cracks.

But there are no cracks in Divine providence. If circumstances had excluded Pinchas, there must have been a good reason. And indeed, there was, because his very exclusion led to the harmonious restructuring of the priesthood.

According to the Sages (*Shemos Rabbah* 7:5; *Bava Basra* 109b),

Pinchas' mother Putiel descended from Joseph and Jethro. Her very name recalled Joseph's resistance to an illicit liaison and Jethro's rejection of idolatry (*Exodus* 6:25; *Rashi*). Moreover, perhaps because Jethro was an outsider, he gave Moses good counsel from a clear perspective (*Exodus* 18:13ff).

Precisely these virtues propelled Pinchas to his heroic deed. Zimri's outrageous act aroused Pinchas' visceral rejection of lust and idolatry. And as an outsider, excluded from the Kehunah, he could observe his relatives the Kohanim treating the people with great love but insufficient zeal. He compensated for their deficiencies when he grabbed his spear and wrought God's vengeance on the sinners. By his heroic deed, Pinchas entered the Kehunah on the highest level, as the beneficiary of God's eternal covenant of harmonious peace.

iii. Joshua and the Sacrifices

MOSES, AWARE THAT HE WILL NOT LEAD THE JEWISH PEOPLE into the Holy Land, asked God to appoint a suitable successor to the leadership position, and God responds by designating Joshua. Then God interjects a seemingly unrelated topic (28:1-2). "And God spoke to Moses, saying, 'Command the children of Israel and say to them: My offering, My food for My fires, My satisfying aroma, you shall be diligent to offer this to Me in its appointed time.' " The Torah then enumerates the obligatory sacrifices of the Sabbath and the festivals. Why insert these particular laws of sacrifices here?

Rashi, quoting from the Midrash (*Sifrei*), suggests a connection between Moses' request for a successor and the sacrifices. "'Rather than command Me [to appoint a new leader for] My children, command My children about Me.' It can be compared to a dying princess who cautioned her husband, 'Take care of my children.' He replied, 'Rather than caution me about my children, caution them about me and tell them not to disobey me and to treat me disrespectfully.' So did the Holy Blessed One say to Moses, 'Rather than caution Me about My children, caution My children about Me, not to treat Me disrespectfully, nor exchange My Honor for foreign gods.' "

At first glance, the Midrash outlines only a general connection between Moses' expression of concern for the people in his absence and God's commands regarding the sacrifices. If God is to be concerned for them, they would have to be concerned about their obligations to Him. But the Midrash does not seem to explain the more specific connection between Moses' request for a worthy successor and the Sabbath and festival sacrifices.

The key to the deeper intent in the Midrash may lie in its judicious use of the first person possessive pronoun. In the parable, the dying princess refers to the children as "my" children. In the husband's rejoinder, he redirects the relationship of the children to himself, not referring to them as "your" children but as "my" children; he reassures her that the children are not only hers but his as well.

Similarly, Moses expressed his concern for the Jewish people and asked God for a successor. God granted the request, and then he spoke to Moses reassuringly of the obligations of "My" children. Specifically, He told Moses to convey to the Jewish people the laws of the sacrifices, because they carry a message of reassurance. The theme of all the festivals is God's continual providence, nationally and individually. God assured the immediate future of the Jewish people by the appointment of the worthy Joshua as successor to the leadership, but even more important, God's perpetual providence, as represented by the festival sacrifices, would provide the ultimate guidance for the nation through all its history.

פרשת מטות
Parashas Mattos

i. A Matter of Vows

AFTER THE DEBACLE OF ZIMRI, IN WHICH THE MIDIANITE women ensnared the Jewish men, God tells Moses to harass and crush Midian. But before this war takes place, the Torah veers off on several tangents, including the appointment of Joshua as Moses' successor and the laws regarding the nullification of a woman's vows. Only then does the Torah return to the business at hand, the campaign against Midian (31:1-2), "And God spoke to Moses, saying, 'Take vengeance for the children of Israel against the Midianites.' "

How are laws concerning a woman's vows so germane that they warrant interrupting so conspicuously the natural flow of the story of the war with Midian?

Essentially, these laws restrict a woman's ability to make unilateral vows. The husband or the father of an unmarried woman can, with certain qualifications, annul them. The deeper premise that underpins these laws is a profound concept about a woman's relationship to the home of her birth and the home of her making. The home is not an entity external to her with which she is involved. Rather, it ideally becomes an essential part of a woman's identity. Her sanctified role emerges in the greater framework of her home into which she integrates herself. The head of the home, be it her father or her husband, is thus intimately involved as a partner in all her affairs that may have bearing on the conduct of the home. Consequently, he has the right to object to any vows that interfere in those areas that relate to the home and annul them.

Had Zimri had this profound understanding of the special qualities and role of the Jewish woman, perhaps he would never have consorted with the Midianite princess. It is certain that Zimri offered some justification for his actions. Perhaps he claimed he was trying to form an alliance with Midian. He rationalized his physical lust to himself until he actually believed he would be drawing Midian into the Jewish orbit as a satellite of the enlarged tent of the Torah community, thereby fulfilling God's final plan for all mankind. He may have compared himself to Moses who had embraced the *eiruv rav*, the Egyptian rabble who joined the Jewish people in the Exodus. The Midianites had already been excluded from full integration with the Jewish nation, but Zimri may have hoped to include them in a diminished role. If so, the Midianite women would have become concubines.[1]

In order to highlight the error of Zimri's rationalization before the actual confrontation with Midian, the Torah presents the laws of vows, which reveal the deeper concept of Jewish womanhood. The ideal role and path of perfection for a Jewish woman lies in her selfless dedication to the home and, by extension, in her selfless submission to the will of the Creator. The Midianite women, products of an idolatrous and cruel culture, could not aspire to

---

1. These events occurred after the Jews had enjoyed an idyllic existence in the desert, learning Torah and drawing ever closer to God for thirty-eight years. It is, therefore, inconceivable that Zimri and his followers did not have some justification for their acts. Perhaps the superficial similarity of their rationale to Moses' inclusion of the *eiruv rav* may explain why specifically Moses forgot certain relevant laws during this crisis.

such a life, and therefore, they had no place in Jewish society, not as wives, not even as concubines.

In this light, we can better understand God's command that the Jewish people not only attack but also harass the Midianites. Doing so would create an abiding antipathy and prevent them from ever again attempting to merge with and corrupt the Jewish people.

ii. Forbidden Dishes

IN THE AFTERMATH OF THE JEWISH VICTORY OVER MIDIAN, Aaron's son Elazar, successor to the office of Kohen Gadol, instructed the people to purify the captured vessels by removing absorbed forbidden foods and immersing them in a *mikveh* (31:22-23). "Only the gold and silver, the copper, the iron, the tin and the lead [vessels], everything that comes into fire, shall you pass through fire, and it will be purified, but it must be purified with the water of sprinkling; and everything that does not come through fire, you shall pass through water."

A simple question arises. The battle against Midian was not the first the Jewish people fought as they approached the Holy Land. They had already fought and defeated the lands of Arad, the Amorites and Bashan (21:1-35). It is reasonable to assume that they captured vessels in those campaigns as well. Why then didn't the Torah use any of those opportunities to introduce the requirement to purify and immerse vessels obtained from non-Jews?

One of the most important benefits of these requirements is to distinguish between Jewish and non-Jewish ownership of food utensils. Along these lines, our Sages forbade non-Jewish foodstuffs, such as wine (*stam yeinam*), bread (*pas*), milk (*chalav*) and cooked food (*bishul*), even when there is no question of non-kosher ingredients. In all these cases, our Sages sought to prevent excessive fraternization between Jew and non-Jew. Breaking bread together is an important aspect of socializing and naturally fosters identification. Hence, the prohibitions against shared food are important barriers against assimilation.

In this light, we can understand why the Torah introduces the law of vessel purification at this point. Unlike Arad, the Amorites or Bashan, with whom there had never been any prospect of fraternization, the first encounter of the Jewish people with Midian had been friendly. Unfortunately, these social relationships quickly strengthened and led to idolatry and debauchery. It was specifically here that the danger of excessive socializing became clear, and it is specifically here, where we can best absorb it, that the Torah teaches this lesson.

iii. *Who Mentioned Menasheh?*

THE JEWISH PEOPLE STOOD ON THE THRESHOLD OF THE Holy Land. They had captured all the lands of the Amorites in Trans-Jordan and were now poised to cross the river into Canaan. The tribes of Gad and Reuven now approached Moses and asked to take their portion in the rich pastureland of the Trans-Jordan (32:1ff). Moses looked askance at their request, but agreed to it provided they met certain conditions. He then divided the newly conquered lands among (32:33) "Gad, Reuven and part of the tribe of Menasheh."

Who mentioned Menasheh?

Only Gad and Reuven had approached Moses; Menasheh did not accompany them. Why then, as the Ramban asks, did Moses include Menasheh among the recipients of land in the Trans-

Jordan? Furthermore, why did Moses split the tribe of Menasheh, giving some of them land in the Trans-Jordan and the rest in Israel proper?

After the deportation of the Ten Lost Tribes and the demise of the northern kingdom centuries later, the tribes of Judah and Benjamin accounted for most of the remaining population of Israel, although elements of the other tribes had migrated south over the years. Providentially, the remnant of the Jewish people represented both matriarchs, Leah and Rachel, the respective forebears of Judah and Benjamin.

When Moses decided to apportion the lands of the Trans-Jordan to Gad and Reuven, he wanted to create the same balance in this extended area of the land of Israel. Since Gad and Reuven both descended from Leah, he wanted to balance their presence with a tribe descended from Rachel. He chose Menasheh, but only part of it. Menasheh, never having asked to settle in the Trans-Jordan, deserved to share in Israel proper along with the other tribes. Therefore, Moses delegated only part of the tribe to settle in the Trans-Jordan. Furthermore, by having one tribe straddle both sides of the Jordan, the group living in the Trans-Jordan, as a whole, would have a familial connection to the heartland. This would cement the link between the two parts of Israel.

The question remains, why choose Menasheh? Moses could have chosen any of three tribes descended from Rachel — Benjamin, Ephraim and Menasheh. Why Menasheh?

We can easily explain Benjamin's exclusion. This tribe was destined to have the Temple in his territory, the place on earth reflecting God's oneness. Moses may have considered it inappropriate to have any fissure in their territory; it had to remain fully contiguous. As for Ephraim, it would be Joshua the Ephraimite who would lead the conquest of Canaan, and it was important that the people have full confidence in his personal commitment to the conquest. Had Ephraim already partially settled in the Trans-Jordan, people might have lost a measure of confidence in Joshua's commitment. Therefore, as a practical matter, Moses selected Menasheh as the best candidate among the three tribes descended from Rachel.

On a deeper level, Menasheh may perhaps have been most suited for the role of establishing a presence from Rachel in the Trans-Jordan. In Joseph's naming of Menasheh (*Genesis* 41:51), he acknowledged that all the hardship he had endured in his separation from home and family (*galus*) would yet find eternal value. The tribe that joined Gad and Reuven would be separated from the rest of the Jewish people who lived in Israel proper. They would face their own trials and threats outside the natural boundaries of Israel without the reassuring presence of all the other tribes nearby or proximity of the Temple. Therefore, Moses chose Menasheh, whose name reflected the abiding trust in God that its patriarch Joseph had expressed when providence had separated him from his family.

פרשת מסעי
Parashas Masei

i. The High Priest's Death

SOMEONE IS CHOPPING WOOD IN THE FOREST. HE SWINGS his axe, the blade comes loose, and it flies off and kills a person standing nearby. How do we deal with this inadvertent killer? The Torah commands that we judge, convict and banish him to one of the *arei miklat*, the designated cities of refuge (35:25). "And he shall dwell in it until the death of the Kohen Gadol."

The Talmud (*Makkos* 11b) points out that the death of the Kohen Gadol presiding at the time of the killing does not liberate the banished killer. Rather, it is the death of the one who presides at the time of the conviction that effects the liberation. When this Kohen Gadol dies, the killer is free to return home. The Talmud then explains that the killer's term of banishment depends on the death of the Kohen Gadol because he should have prayed that the killer be exonerated.

A number of questions immediately come to mind. Why is the Kohen Gadol obligated to pray for the exoneration of an accused killer? What if the accused is actually guilty? Why should he have prayed for the killer to escape his deserved punishment? Moreover, why does the killer's banishment hinge on the life and death of the Kohen Gadol in office at the time of his conviction? We could have made a case for a connection to the Kohen Gadol who presided at the time of the killing; perhaps he, as the role model of love and brotherhood, bore some responsibility for a crime that took place on his watch, so to speak. But why attach blame to the Kohen Gadol present only at the time of the trial and conviction?

There are two categories of inadvertent killers. One is called *oness*, which means that the killer had absolutely no control over his actions; for instance, if he was pushed off a roof, fell on a child and killed him. In such circumstances, the killer bears no responsibility whatsoever. The other is called *shogeg*, which means the act resulted from an avoidable carelessness. The Torah holds this killer accountable for his irresponsibility and banishes him to a city of refuge, just as the Torah holds the inadvertent (*shogeg*) violator accountable for other commandments to the extent that they require sacrificial atonement.

Why does God demand that we banish a person for neglecting to secure the blade of an axe? Certainly, he had no intention or desire to kill anyone. Perhaps he didn't even know the victim was standing nearby.

The Torah reveals profound psychological truths concerning the structure of the human psyche that are only recently being discovered by modern psychology. Beneath our conscious awareness, there exists a vast hidden universe of drives and motivations that is partially revealed in our dreams, slips of the tongue and other seeming accidents; there are, however, no accidents to the unconscious. Therefore, the Torah holds people responsible for unintentional avoidable violations.

In the case of accidental killing, for instance, the killer undoubtedly knew at some level that using that defective axe could cause grievous injury or even death, and yet he did not refrain from using it. Perhaps some latent hostility or other aggressive tendency acted as a countervailing force to block or repress this awareness from his conscious thoughts, which might have horrified him had he considered the potential consequences of his actions. Nonetheless, it is a person's responsibility to discover and control these subconscious forces, to either resist them or expunge them from his psyche if possible. Man is accountable for all the damage he causes in the interim.

The banishment of the inadvertent killer to a city of refuge protects him from blood-avenging relatives, but it also helps him correct the faults and shortcomings that led to his actions. In his place of confinement, he may contemplate his condition, examine his inner self and effect changes. Furthermore, the parameters of his banishment steer him toward a proper examination of his failings. By decreeing that the killer remain there until the death of the Kohen Gadol, the Torah puts him in a bind. His release now depends on the death of the Kohen Gadol, a man completely innocent, holy, righteous and devoted to peace. The inadvertent killer may then recoil in horror as he finds himself thinking about or even wishing for the Kohen Gadol's death. When this happens, his previously unrecognized cavalier attitude toward human life, which has already resulted in one innocent's death, becomes revealed. This is the path to repentance.

Now we can understand why the inadvertent killer is liberated by the death of the Kohen Gadol presiding at the time of his conviction rather than at the time of the killing. The conviction and its consequences declare to the accused that he is responsible for what he has wrought and that he needs to repent. He now needs to search the forces of his unconscious to discover what led to his terrible act. It is now that the Torah challenges him by making his freedom dependent on the death of the presiding Kohen Gadol. The death of the Kohen Gadol who served prior to his conviction does not carry the same meaning in his program of self-examination.

Nonetheless, we still need to explain why the Torah places the

Kohen Gadol in this difficult position of vulnerability to the prayers of killers or their families. The Talmud states that the Kohen Gadol's mother customarily sent gifts to the exiled murderers and their families so that they shouldn't pray for his untimely demise. As mentioned, the Talmud finds fault with him in that he did not pray sufficiently for a verdict of innocence. The Kohen Gadol, unlike the judges who seek justice, is not meant to be neutral; he is the defender of the people (*saneigor*), the one who enters the Holy of Holies on Yom Kippur to plead for their complete expiation from sin. Therefore, the Talmud finds justice in this law; the Kohen Gadol failed to mount an adequate defense for the man accused of inadvertent murder.

ii. Geopolitical Concerns

MEMBERS OF MENASHEH SPOTTED A PROBLEM WITH THE apportionment of the land (36:1ff). A man named Tzelaphchad had died leaving five unmarried daughters but no sons. Would they inherit in place of their father? And if they did, wouldn't the tribal lands of Menasheh be lost if these women later married into another tribe? Furthermore, tribal leaders worried that from that point on those lands would always revert to their descendants in the other tribe when the Jubilee year (*Yovel*) arrived; they would no longer belong to Menasheh.

Moses acknowledged their concerns and instructed the daughters of Tzelaphchad to marry only within their own tribe. It is well known, however, that there was never any restraint on tribal intermarriage throughout Jewish history. The Talmud (*Bava Basra* 120a) states that Moses had restricted intermarriage only until the conquest and apportionment of Canaan, which were completed fourteen years later.

A question still remains. If the restriction against tribal intermarriage lasted only fourteen short years, how did Moses address Menasheh's concerns about tribal lands shifting to other tribes every fiftieth (Jubilee) year? Any intermarriage during the first fifty years following the conquest of Israel might result in just such a transference during the first Jubilee (*Yovel*) year.

Perhaps we may suggest that Menasheh was primarily concerned with tribal boundaries rather than tribal ownership. The division of the land among the tribes resulted in a federal or provincial system, wherein each tribe constituted its own political entity, which together with its counterparts formed the tribal federation of Israel. The tribe of Menasheh was concerned that if Tzelaphchad's daughters married out of the tribe before the division of the land, their inheritance would be integrated into the political entity of their husbands' tribes, thereby diminishing the apportionment and the geopolitical position of Menasheh. By forbidding such intermarriage until the conquest and division were complete, Moses ensured that all Menasheh's tribal lands would remain within their borders; the political status of the lands would not be affected, just as a Texan owning land in New York does not make that land part of Texas.

Menasheh had expressed concern about the reversion of lands during the first and subsequent Jubilee years. Moses' temporary ban on tribal intermarriage addressed this concern. Once Joshua would set the provincial borders of each tribe, the ancestral boundaries of Menasheh would be fixed forevermore, reflecting God's providence in the apportionment of the land.

דברים
DEUTERONOMY

פרשת דברים
Parashas Devarim

i. *A Subtle Rebuke*

ONE MIGHT HAVE EXPECTED A ROUSING ORATORICAL OVERture to introduce the final book of the Torah, which is almost entirely the last words spoken by Moses to the Jewish people just before he died. Instead, it opens with seemingly irrelevant geographical information (1:1-2): "These are the words Moses spoke to all Israel on the other side of the Jordan in the desert, in the Aravah, opposite Suf, between Parran, Tofel, Lovan, Chatzeros and Di Zahav. Eleven days journey from Sinai by way of Mount Se'ir until Kadesh Barnei'a."

Rashi, quoting from the *Sifrei,* explains that these locales cryptically refer to the most egregious sins of the nation during their forty years in the desert. For instance, Di Zahav (a play on words for *die zahav*, enough gold) subtly alludes to the construction of the Golden Calf, which the Jews had cast from their excess gold thirty-nine years earlier.

Why did Moses use these oblique references instead of more explicit ones? Rashi explains that Moses clothes his criticism in innocuous terms out of respect for the sensibilities of the Jewish people; they would have recoiled from more direct criticism.

A question immediately arises. A brief glance at the first few chapters of the Book of Deuteronomy reveals explicit and extensive rebukes to the nation for these very sins, and Moses does not mince words in his harsh criticism. In fact, reproach is a recurrent and major theme of the Torah's final Book. Why then are his references so veiled in the first two verses?

Moses reveals here a sensitivity to an important aspect of human psychology. People do not like to confront their own faults, and they certainly resent having others call them to their attention. The instinctive response to chastisement is withdrawal. In order to deflect this reflexive response and gently guide the people toward self-scrutiny, Moses initially used oblique references to hint at the sins.

When the people heard him mention Di Zahav, they thought, "A place where we had a lot of gold? Oh, that was when we made the Golden Calf." Then they directed their thoughts on their own to that awful tragedy, initiating the process of honest introspection. Afterward, when Moses spoke of it directly, they were no longer so resistant and defensive.

With deep insight into the dynamics of rebuke, Moses had effectively prepared the Jewish people to accept reproach with an open mind and an open heart. And he simultaneously instructed all future generations in how to give such rebuke.

ii. *Rare Qualifications*

IT TOOK MOSES NEARLY A YEAR TO FOLLOW HIS father-in-law Jethro's advice, and even then, he appears to have missed important details. When Jethro came from Midian to join the Jewish people, who had just emerged from Egypt, he saw Moses overburdened by judicial duties and advised him to appoint qualified judges to share the load (*Exodus* 18:13ff).

How do we define "qualified judges"? According to Jethro, they should be "God-fearing, men of truth and haters of greed." But in our *parashah*, forty years later, Moses reports that he actually sought other qualifications a year after Jethro offered his advice (1:13), "Righteous men, wise, insightful, well known to their tribes." There is no mention of the three qualities Jethro advocated. Moses further reports that he found only three of these four qualifications (1:15). He did not find "insightful men."

Why couldn't Moses find men with this quality? Moreover, why did Moses ignore the three qualifications Jethro had specified?

The Midrash (*Sifrei* 13:15) explains that Jethro had actually presented Moses with all seven qualifications, only three of which the Torah records in the Book of Exodus. This *parashah* reveals the others, of which Moses could actually find only three.

Questions still remain. Why didn't the Torah credit Jethro for the entirety of his advice? Furthermore, our Sages considered the Jewish people who lived and thrived in the desert as the *dor dei'ah*, the generation of knowledge. How then is it possible that Moses could not find these virtues among the people? If Moses could not find among them judges with all seven qualifications, how could we ever hope to do so in the future?

It seems reasonable to assume that Jethro emphasized some qualifications more than others — the three mentioned in his name. He stressed those he considered most difficult to find — God-fearing, men of truth and haters of greed. These traits were somehow different, and the Torah records Jethro's emphasis.

History validated Jethro's fears. Moses was not able to find men who had Jethro's three special qualifications. In fact, he could not even find men who had all four of the more ordinary qualifications. His final choices had only three qualifications, "righteous, well-known and wise," but not "insightful." Why indeed was it impossible for Moses to find men who were God-fearing, lovers of truth, haters of greed and insightful?

Let us refine the question. Undoubtedly, there were many men who possessed a considerable measure of these virtues. We must surmise, therefore, that Jethro and Moses sought individuals completely exemplary in these traits, beyond even a hint of reproach. Still, why could none be found?

The answer lies in the background of the Jewish people at the time of the Exodus. They had just emerged from two hundred and ten years of captivity in Egypt, and they had not yet developed the cultural institutions that could consistently produce men outstanding in these character virtues.

Moses discovered that they could produce wise men but not insightful ones. Wisdom (*chochmah*) is the ability to grasp the totality of an idea, while insight (*binah*) is the ability to make deductions and discern all its fine distinctions and detail. Insight develops in an intellectual environment through the process of *shakla v'taria*, the give and take of dynamic argumentation. For nearly two hundred years, the Egyptians had oppressed and enslaved the Jewish people. An environment of precise intellectual thought is the luxury of a free and unburdened people, not people whose lives are precariously balanced on the edge. The emancipated Jews had not yet had the opportunity to create a culture that fosters such intellectual acuity. They could grasp the basic concepts of Torah and its laws, but they were not practiced enough in rigorous thought to produce leaders renowned for their ability to penetrate to all the Torah's intricacies.

Moses also discovered that they could produce righteous men, as Rashi defines the word *anashim*, but not God-fearing ones. Righteous people pursue fairness and justice, but absolute fear of God develops from a constant awareness of His providence and judgment. Fear of God arises when His judgments are most manifest. For two centuries, the Egyptians wickedly oppressed the Jews, and God's justice remained hidden. Fear of

God declined. The Exodus, with all its miracles and wonders, proved to the Jewish people intellectually that God's judgment was present, but the reconditioning of hearts takes a much longer time. One year after the Exodus, this trait of God-fearing was not yet so deeply rooted in the nation as a whole that it could produce sterling examples as judges.

Hatred of greed is also a sentiment that takes root only after a culture reaches a state of maturity. When a society becomes prosperous, it no longer needs to concern itself with the basic necessities of life but may now pursue the materialistic luxuries. These pursuits, however, do not provide any meaningful or lasting satisfaction, only negative consequences. At that point, intelligent people tend to become repelled by greed and turn away from materialism. The Jewish people, just one year after emancipation from two centuries of oppression and privation, had not yet had sufficient experience to develop this sophistication, a responsive revulsion to greed.

Finally, there is the qualification of "men of truth." In his *Guide to the Perplexed*, the Rambam writes that Moses could not have become the great prophet and leader of the Jewish people had he been brought up as a slave, as were his brethren. Only as a prince in Pharaoh's palace, completely removed from the burdens of slavery, could he achieve his uniquely elevated state of intellect. In the oppressive environment of slavery, man's daily existence hangs by a thread, and the luxury of the pursuit of truth as an end in itself is a casualty. Jethro understood this and likewise emphasized this virtue. And indeed, it was impossible to find "men of truth" in the fullest sense of the word among the emancipated Jewish slaves.

In later generations, however, the Jewish people did develop a society based on personal liberty and a strong intellectual tradition. Eventually, there was no shortage of candidates for the judiciary who were not only righteous, renowned and wise but also insightful, God-fearing, lovers of truth and haters of greed.

iii. The Five Books of Moses

ALTHOUGH THE TORAH COULD EASILY HAVE BEEN merged into one Book, it is subdivided into the Five Books of Moses, otherwise known as the *Chumash* or Pentateuch, "the set of five" in Hebrew and Greek respectively. Kabbalistic writings discuss extensively the number five's metaphysical significance and draw a correlation between the five realms of creation and the five Books of the Torah. Be that as it may, the division of the Torah into separate Books indicates that each has a distinct and identifiable theme. What are these themes?

Perhaps we can find an allusion to them in the famous first Mishnah of the Tractate *Pe'ah*. Every morning, after we make the blessing concerning Torah study, we immediately study this Mishnah, which states, "These are the commandments that are performed without measure: leaving the corner of the field for the poor (*pe'ah*), bringing first fruits (*bikkurim*), making a regular appearance at the Temple (*ra'yon*), bestowing kindness on others (*gemilus chassadim*) and the study of Torah (*talmud Torah*)."

We may find that these five commandments correspond to the Five Books of Moses, and a close examination of this relationship illuminates their common themes. Let us examine one pair at a time.

The overriding theme of Genesis is creation, beginning with the creation of the universe and culminating with the creation of the fledgling Jewish nation. Among the thorniest questions in Jewish thought is: How can anything exist outside of God when there is no necessary reality outside of Him (*ein od milvado*)? The Kabbalistic response is the concept of Divine contraction (*tzimtzum*). Simplistically stated, God contract His will, so to speak, to create a realm where it is not utterly manifest, thereby allowing for the creation of the universe.[1] In this regard, *pe'ah* can be considered a metaphor for creation. *Pe'ah* emerges only when the Jewish landowner removes or withdraws the harvested crop and thereby makes the corner of his field available to the poor and landless. The first Book then corresponds to the first commandment mentioned in the Mishnah.

Exodus describes the emergence of the Jewish people from Egypt as a nation dedicated to fulfilling the Divine will. We commemorate this seminal event by bringing the first fruits of the harvest to the Temple. This is the second commandment mentioned in the Mishnah. Upon his arrival there, the landowner declares his total gratitude to God (25:5ff). In his recital, he recalls the emancipation and redemption of the Jewish people from physical and moral bondage in Egypt; this text subsequently formed the backbone of the Passover Haggadah. Furthermore, on the occasion of bringing the first fruits (*bikkurim*), the Jew recalls God's relationship with the Jewish people, whom He calls His firstborn (*bechor*). The Book of Leviticus, which our Sages also called *Toras Kohanim* (the Priestly Code), focuses primarily on the priestly duties and the Divine service in the Tabernacle and in the Temple afterward. This corresponds clearly to the third commandment on the Mishnah's list, the obligation to come and bring sacrifices in the Temple (*ra'yon*).

The Book of Numbers, the fourth in the Torah, chronicles the Jewish experience during the four decades spent in the desert, the trials and tribulations, triumphs and setbacks. These travails culminate at the Book's conclusion when the people stand poised to enter the land.

What salient feature characterizes the people? It is the same virtue that abided in them when they received the Torah. The success of the Jewish people at Mount Sinai can be encapsulated in

---

1. This is, by necessity, an oversimplified and inadequate description of the concept of *tzimtzum*. It must be understood that God, in His perfection, is unchanging; creation results from His acts, not His essence. Perhaps the Arizal chose the descriptive term of *tzimtzum* with regard to God and His creation because it so obviously cannot be understood in any literal sense. For an extensive discussion, see *Nefesh HaChaim*, chapter 3.

the word *vayichan*, as it appears in the phrase (*Exodus* 19:2), "The people of Israel encamped (*vayichan*) by the mountain." Why does the Torah use the singular form of the verb (*vayichan*) when the plural (*vayachanu*) would seem grammatically correct? The *Mechilta* explains that they encamped as "one body, with one heart."

The unity among the Jewish people at Sinai, which reflected the unity of God (cf. Shabbos afternoon liturgy), was an essential prerequisite for entry into the land, and the efforts to foster and maintain it characterize the Jewish sojourn in the desert. And the most effective vehicle for unity is unselfish kindness, the fourth commandment in the Mishnah. This assessment is reinforced by the prophet, who recalls the importance and centrality of kindness among the Jewish people in the desert (*Jeremiah* 2:2), "I [God] remember the kindness of your youth, when you walked after Me in the desert."

Finally, we come to the Book of Deuteronomy. The *Zohar* comments that Deuteronomy, also called *Mishneh Torah* (repetition of the Torah), corresponds to the Oral Law. Indeed, it differs from the other Books in content and style, often repeating laws taught earlier. According to our Sages, "the Divine Presence spoke the first four Books from Moses' throat," while Moses composed the fifth with a perfectly rarefied Divine inspiration. The fifth commandment of the Mishnah, the obligation to study Torah, hence corresponds to Deuteronomy's theme.

Perhaps we can discern a subtle teaching in the Mishnah's connection of the commandments to the Five Books of Moses. Ordinarily, a person performing a commandment is exempt from other commandments that may present themselves while he is so occupied. A person learning Torah, however, is granted no such exemption. This is perplexing, especially since our Sages consider Torah study comparable to all the other commandments combined. Rav Yitzchak Hutner, in *Pachad Yitzchak* (Shavuos), explains that a person who interrupts his studies to perform a commandment actually fulfills the commandment of Torah study; Torah study is meant to lead to performance. By highlighting five limitless commandments that correspond to the five themes of the Torah, the Mishnah teaches us that study and performance are completely intertwined, that the commandments themselves bring us to greater knowledge of God and the perfection to which we aspire.

In light of our discussion of the Book of Genesis, we gain new insight into the blessing we recite after we void our wastes. In it, we laud God Who "formed (*yatzar*) man in wisdom and created (*bara*) in him orifices and hollows." In Hebrew usage, creation refers to producing something from nothing, *ex nihilo*, while formation means the reconfiguration of existing materials. Why then are man's orifices and hollows "created" when he himself is only described as "formed"?

Modern physics confirms the ancient wisdom of our mystic masters that space has no inherent existence; it is a byproduct of the creation of matter/energy. Thus, space is a creation. When God "contracted" His presence, using the Kabbalistic anthropomorphism, He created space *ex nihilo*, a creation from nothing. We, therefore, refer in our blessing to the placement of the empty spaces in man's body with the language of creation. It is a subtle reminder that space itself is a result of the prototypal act of creation.

iv. *Fearing Fear Is Still Fear*

THE DISASTROUS INCIDENT OF THE SPIES CONDEMNED the Jewish people to wander in the desert for four decades. Forty years later, Moses again chastised the people for their reluctance to enter the land. Moses recalls how they responded then, how they tried to turn back the clock. Moses reminds them (1:41-44), "Then you spoke and said to me, 'We sinned to

God. We shall go out and do battle according to everything God, our Lord, has commanded us.' Every man girded his weapons of war and prepared to ascend the mountain. And God said to me, 'Tell them not to ascend nor do battle, for I am not among you.'... But you rebelled against God's word and you were willful and climbed the mountain. The Amorites who dwell on that mountain went out against you and pursued you as the bees would do..." This ill-fated adventure thirty-nine years earlier ended in further disaster, as the Amorites slaughtered many in the ensuing battle.

How are we to understand the actions of these people who went to war? Moses had just told them explicitly in the Name of God that they would not succeed. Did they expect to be victorious without God on their side? Furthermore, what is the Torah trying to teach us by comparing the Amorite pursuers to swarming bees? What purpose does this simile serve?

These brave but misguided souls were the very same people who had just been frightened off by the spies' tale of huge Canaanite defenders next to whom they had felt like grasshoppers and over whom they would have prevailed with God's help (*Numbers* 13:33). They failed to listen to Joshua and Caleb, the only spies to make favorable reports. Fear overcame them. When God decreed that the Jewish people would have to remain in the desert, these Jews drew the wrong conclusion. They identified their fear as the villain, the cause of their banishment from the land. Embarrassed by their cowardice, they vowed to fight and prove their bravery. In that state of mind, they could not consider Moses' warnings, to do so would only confirm what they thought was their fatal sin — fear. They would have none of it, and they marched defiantly into battle.

In reality, it was not their fear that caused their downfall following the spies' report but their lack of faith. There is no shame in the fear of death; avoiding mortal battle is more a sign of reason than of cowardice. Their failure stemmed from their inadequate relationship with God. Had they enjoyed a stronger faith, they would have confidently expected to conquer Canaan with

God's help, as indeed Caleb told them they would; there was no rational reason to fear.

Why didn't they share Caleb's confidence? Probably because they were unsure of their own commitment to keeping the Torah when they would enter the land. Consequently, deep in their hearts they did not expect God to protect them.

Unfortunately, they failed to understand the root cause of their punishment — their lack of faith and commitment. Instead, they identified it as fear. When they heard the first clang of swords in battle, their already fearful hearts melted again, and they fled in terror. The Amorites pursued them like bees, measure for measure for their sin. They had refused to face what they perceived as the gigantic Canaanite defenders over whom they would have prevailed with God's help. In return, they were ignominiously vanquished and slaughtered by foes compared to minuscule bees.

Prior to their entry into the land thirty-nine years later, Moses carefully reminded the people of the root cause of their earlier failure.

v. *No More, No Less*

ASK MOST PEOPLE IF THEY WOULD LIKE TO HAVE more rules governing their lives, and they will undoubtedly decline the offer. It is human nature. People instinctively avoid new burdens and restrictions. If anything, they are inclined to disencumber themselves from the burdens and restrictions they already have.

Let us now look at Moses' instructions to the Jewish people (4:2), "You shall not add to that which I command you, nor shall you subtract from it." First, he admonished them not to add and only afterwards not to subtract. Shouldn't he have presented these instructions in the reverse order? First, he should have warned them not to subtract any rules, as they might be inclined to do, and then not to add any rules, which was unlikely to happen in any case. Indeed, history has shown us that Jewish schismatic movements that abrogated the restrictions of the law attracted the most followers and had the greatest longevity. Didn't this type of eventuality present the greatest danger Moses had to anticipate? Why did Moses reverse the order?

A close inspection of the Book of Deuteronomy reveals a number of anomalies. All the Books of the Bible following Genesis begin with a conjunction (the letter *vav*) connecting them to the previous Book — except for Deuteronomy. This suggests that, in some sense, Deuteronomy stands alone. Moreover, in structure and literary style, Deuteronomy speaks from Moses' personal perspective.

Our Sages explain that the first four Books were the direct word of the Divine Presence speaking from Moses' throat (*Shechinah medaberes mitoch grono shel Moshe*). Deuteronomy, on the other hand, was spoken by Moses according to his unparalleled and rarefied Divine inspiration. The commentators offer various explanations of the substantive difference between these two forms of prophecy — God "speaking from Moses' throat" and Divine inspiration. In any event, there appears to be a consensus among them that the final Book of the Torah reflects something of the personality or understanding of Moses in its expression.

We see this very clearly when Moses speaks to the people later on (10:12), "And now, O Israel, what does God your Lord ask of you? Only to fear God your Lord, to walk in all His ways, to love Him and to serve God your Lord with all your heart and all your soul." Quite a tall order. The Talmud (*Berachos* 33b) wonders, "Is fear of God such a small thing? Yes, for Moses it was a small thing." Here we see Moses' personal perspective coming through. This perspective would not have been discernible in any of the Books other than Deuteronomy.

Now we can understand why Moses warned the people against adding to the Torah before he warned against subtraction. Once again, it is Moses' personal perspective coming through. For Moses, with his virtually boundless love for God and the Torah, the possibility of subtraction was exceedingly remote. Why would someone want to forgo even one sweet commandment of the Torah? Rather, the risk lay in addition. Moses feared that religious fervor might lead to the formulation of additional commandments by which to connect with God, and therefore, he issued his first warning against addition.

פרשת ואתחנן
Parashas Va'eschanan

i. Derailed Inclinations

Perhaps no words encapsulate a credo for Jewish life better than the *Shema*. We utter them daily when we awake and retire, and at the moment before we draw our last breath. We bind them to our bodies and affix them to the doorposts of our homes. Let us take a closer look at the first obligation it imposes upon us (6:5), "You shall love God your Lord with all your heart."

There are two ways of spelling the word heart, either *lamed veis* (לֵב) or *lamed veis veis* (לֵבָב). In the *Shema*, the Torah uses the double *veis* form. The Talmud (*Berachos* 54a) comments that the extra *veis* whose numerical value is two instructs us that we should love God with both of our hearts, that is to say, both our good and evil inclinations (*yetzer hatov* and *yetzer hara*). It is not difficult to understand the need to redirect man's material and distracting inclinations (*yetzer hara*) to the love of God. But why does God enjoin us to love Him with our good inclinations as well? Isn't it the very nature of the good inclination to love God?

Apparently not. Man indeed has a virtuous impulse that

enables him to step outside his selfish needs and act altruistically, but that is not necessarily identical with loving God. For instance, this impulse can find corrupt expression in a secular humanism battling to achieve legislative legitimacy for alternative lifestyles or a communist seeking to create an atheistic utopian society. These misguided activities are marked by good intentions and even self-sacrifice, but they spawn evil results; they are motivated by derailed inclinations. Man must ground his altruism, his second good heart, in the knowledge and love of God's revealed will.

ii. *The Serpent's Venom*

MOSES REMINDS THE PEOPLE OF THE SEARING IMAGES OF the revelation at Mount Sinai (4:11), "And you approached and stood at the foot of the mountain, and the mountain blazed with fire into the very heart of the heavens." The Talmud (*Shabbos* 145b) states that this seminal experience of Sinai removed from the Jewish people the venom that the serpent had injected into Eve and thereby into all of mankind. What exactly does this mean?

One of the key characteristics that set Jewish people apart from the rest of the world is the conviction that there is a discoverable absolute truth. Unlike the pagan world, as well as modern society to a great degree, which ascribes to moral relativism, accepting multiple truths and consequently no truth, Judaism maintains with full conviction that a discoverable absolute truth exists. Thus the yearning to find truth is deeply imprinted in our national psyche.

Ideally, this desire finds expression in the study of Torah, the fulfillment of its commandments and the forging of a personal relationship with God. But even Jews who have drifted away from Torah are driven by this inner yearning, a cultural expression, and many of them find other modes of expression. Thus we find Jews in the vanguard of the arts, sciences and even revolutionary movements in a proportion that vastly exceeds our numbers in the world.

When was this conviction born in the Jewish psyche? According to the Talmud, it was when the Jewish people experienced God's revelation at Mount Sinai, when they experienced absolute truth in its highest, clearest form. This is the transformation suggested by the metaphor of the serpent's venom. The serpent had convinced Eve that she did not need to heed God's command, that there were other truths in a moral relativist world, but the stand at Mount Sinai dispelled this blunder from the collective Jewish psyche for all time among all Jews who are loyal to their Jewish heritage.

iii. Decapitation and Stoning

ACCORDING TO OUR SAGES, DECAPITATION BY SWORD IS A better death than stoning. It would follow, therefore, that sins punishable by decapitation are not as severe as those punishable by stoning. But is this in fact so?

Among the Ten Commandments, we find two extremely grave sins, Sabbath desecration and murder, both of which are capital offenses. But there is an important difference. We stone the Sabbath desecrator, if properly warned, but we "only" decapitate the murderer. This would imply that Sabbath desecration is more severe than murder. On the other hand, it is permitted to desecrate the Sabbath in order to save a life, but it is forbidden to murder in similar circumstances. This would imply that these two sins are at least of equal severity. If so, why is Sabbath desecration punished more severely?

Upon closer examination, we can distinguish two aspects of a crime. One is the gravity of the offense itself and the physical and spiritual damage it caused. Second is the degree of criminality that went into the performance of the act.

One of the dominant forces of human nature is the aggressive impulse (*kinah*), which forms part of man's *yetzer hara*, his base physical drives. These drives challenge him in his lifelong struggle to achieve holiness. In most instances, a murderer is driven to his act by extreme provocation. Something makes his blood boil, awakens his primitive instincts and sends him into a rage. The murderer loses the struggle to overcome this impulse.

Most often, however, Sabbath desecration is a different story. There are rarely fiery impulses that drive man to desecrate the Sabbath; no overwhelming human drives to turn on a light or to write a letter, both of which are Sabbath violations. The transgressor generally acts for his convenience, indifferent to the Torah or perhaps even chafing at the notion that God restricts his desires. The willful criminality behind this act generally indicates a more profound corruption of the soul in rebellion against God, a criminality greater than that of the murderer.

Our Sages have understood that a central purpose of any punishment, including execution, is to gain the transgressor's penitence so that he may achieve atonement for his eternal soul. Fittingly, the Torah establishes that the Sabbath desecrator receives the greater punishment, for the corruption of his soul calls for a greater atonement.

This is but one of the reasons that Sabbath desecration may receive a more severe punishment. There are also others. Ultimately, all God's commands are the product of His infinite, inscrutable wisdom. Nonetheless, we are obliged to probe the depth of the Torah for its wisdom and, in so doing, draw ever nearer to God.

iv. Sharp Learning

THE FIRST PARAGRAPH OF THE *SHEMA* APPEARS IN THIS *parashah* (6:6-7), "And these matters that I command you today shall be upon your heart. You shall teach them thoroughly to your children and you shall speak of them while you sit in your home, while you travel on the road, when you retire and when you arise."

There are many similarities in the language between this first paragraph of the *Shema* and the second paragraph, which appears in *Parashas Eikev.* In describing our obligation to teach our children, the first paragraph uses the term *shinantam* (וְשִׁנַּנְתָּם). Rashi relates it to the term *shinun*, sharpening, meaning that we should give our children such a "sharp" grasp of Torah that they will answer any question without hesitation. In the second paragraph, the instruction to teach is expressed with the term *limad'tem* (וְלִמַּדְתֶּם) the standard term for teaching.

The different choice of terms can be explained by the pronoun use of the respective paragraphs. The first paragraph addresses the individual, whereas the second paragraph, which uses the plural form, relates to the community as a whole. The community must ensure that there are institutions of learning for all children. However, each individual parent does not discharge his obligation merely by sending his children to *yeshivos*. The Torah requires an extra input from the parents to see that their children's learning is "sharp."

v. Night and Day

NIGHT AND DAY, WE ARE OBLIGATED TO STUDY THE TORAH (6:6-7), "And these matters that I command you today shall be upon your heart. You shall teach them thoroughly to your children, and you shall speak of them while you sit in your home, while you travel on the road, when you retire and when you arise."

The Talmud (Shabbos 127a) discusses those things that bear fruit in this world while the principal lasts into the next. Among these are "early arrival at the house of study mornings and evenings . . . and Torah study is comparable to them all."

The Talmud that directs us to learn day and night seems to be echoing the aforementioned verse in the *Shema* that stresses the importance of learning at daybreak (when one rises) and at night (when one lies down). If so, would it not have been more appropriate to stress the importance of learning late into the night rather than arriving at the house of study early in the evening. Furthermore, how does the requirement for timely arrival in the house of study differ from "Torah study," the commandment mentioned last in the passage from the Talmud?

Daytime is a period of activity and accomplishment, a time when man takes care of his needs and secures his livelihood. Nighttime is a period of passivity when the body and mind rest. During sleep, according to our Sages, the soul detaches somewhat from the body, rendering the experience of sleep one-sixtieth of death.

By shaking free of the nocturnal lassitude and rising early to learn Torah, man expresses the dominion of his higher self over his baser instinctual component. At the opposite end of the day, by going early to learn as night begins, when he enjoys some leisure and the opportunity to pursue various personal interests, man expresses his rejection of physical pleasure or self-aggrandizement; he directs himself rather towards the ultimate pleasure, clinging to God.

Man, therefore, gains in both instances, day and night, when he advances the hour of his Torah study. He enjoys the fruits of his labor now, as he perceives a portion of God's infinite wisdom, and he has the lasting benefit of transforming his soul by breaking its attachments to both the physical and psychological self. In this sense, the Talmud's directives toward Torah study are not redundant. The first speaks of the correct attitude toward learning and the behaviors that stem from it, while the second refers to the value of the learning itself.

When the Torah enjoins us to learn "when we travel on the road," it seems to refer to any and all circumstances, not certain specific ones. Would it then not have been more appropriate to speak of the indefinite "on a road" (*bederech*) rather that the definitive "on the road" (*baderech*)? The use of "the road" implies that there are some roads upon which one should not learn. Perhaps it is suggesting that one should not study Torah on every road. Rather, one should study Torah on "the road" whose goal is to lead one to God. A person who learns Torah in order to find fault with it (*lekanter*) gains no benefit from his learning.

פרשת עקב
Parashas Eikev

i. Hypothetical Error Number Two

MOSES DID NOT WANT THE JEWISH PEOPLE TO GET SWELLED heads when they conquered Canaan; he did not want them to think they deserved all the miracles God was about to perform for them in driving out the indigenous peoples. Standing on the threshold of the Holy Land, he warned them against smugness and complacency (9:4-5).

"Do not say in your heart when God dislodges [the nations] before you, saying, 'By virtue of my righteousness did God bring me to take possession of this land,' and because of the nations' wickedness did God drive them away before you. It is neither your righteousness nor the uprightness of your heart that enables you to come and take possession of their land. Rather, by virtue of the wickedness of these nations, God drives them away before you, and in order to uphold the word God swore to your forefathers — to Abraham, Isaac and Jacob."

Moses begins by presenting a hypothetical error the Jewish people might make, an erroneous statement that he warns them "not to say in their hearts." There are two parts to their hypothetical statement — that their own righteousness entitles them to the land and that the wickedness of the nations causes them to be driven out. The verse suggests that both of these statements should not be "said in their hearts." In other words, they are both wrong.

This is extremely puzzling, for in the very next verse Moses tells them that the wickedness of the nations will indeed cause them to be driven out. Apparently, there was only one error, the attribution of the conquest to their own righteousness rather than the righteousness of their forefathers. Why then does the Torah give the impression that the entire hypothetical statement is erroneous?

In actuality, there is an important difference between the hypothetical explanation for the fate of the nations and the correct view Moses presented. In the hypothetical statement, the Jews mention their own virtue first and only then the wickedness of the nations as the reason for their ejection. The impression is that the Jewish people gain the right to the land by virtue of their relatively superior righteousness.

The implication here is that the fate of the nations depends on the relative Jewish position. If God finds the Jews lacking in righteousness, the nations are to remain in place. But if God finds them more righteous, He will give them the land and drive out the nations.

Not so, declares Moses, and he reverses the order. First, he mentions the wickedness of the nations and only afterward does he mention the supposed righteousness of the Jews. The point is clear. The banishment of the nations from the land is entirely independent of the Jewish people's relative righteousness and their ability to conquer the land. God consecrates the land with His presence and providence; in the land, His justice is manifest. The land is too holy to tolerate the indefinite presence of the corrupt Canaanite nations. Regardless of whether or not the Jews earn the right to enter, God will drive out the iniquitous nations. This was hypothetical error number one. Interestingly, before the large influx of Jews over the past century, the land of Israel had lain barren and denuded for two millennia, depopulated of iniquitous nations that could lay false claim to it.

Hypothetical error number two relates to the Jewish people's right to the land. It is not by virtue of their own righteousness, Moses tells them, but in the merit of their forefathers to whom God had promised the land.

ii. The Mystery of the Fourth Blessing

OF ALL THE BLESSINGS WE MAKE DAILY, THE TORAH SPECIFically mandates only *Birchas HaMazon,* the Grace after Meals (8:10), "And you shall eat and be satisfied, and you shall bless God your Lord for the land He has given you."

Birchas HaMazon is actually composed of four blessings. According to the Talmud (*Berachos* 48b), the Torah indisputably mandates the first three. There is, however, a difference of opinion as to whether the fourth blessing is a Biblical law (*mi'd'oraysa*) or a Rabbinic enactment (*mi'd'rabbanan*).

The Talmud goes on to identify the authors of the various blessings. Moses composed the first, Joshua the second, David and Solomon the third and the Sages of Yavneh the fourth following the Roman siege of Beitar.

We can well understand how the first and second blessings, being that they were composed in the desert, are considered Biblical requirements. We are somewhat perplexed by the

Talmud's assertion that the third blessing, composed by David and Solomon some five hundred years later, is considered a Biblical requirement. This question, however, can be resolved without too much difficulty. Although Solomon constructed the Temple centuries after the giving of the Torah, the concept of a centralized place of worship already existed. The Jewish people in the desert had a *Mishkan* (Tabernacle), and God also instructed them there concerning the future construction of a Temple in the Holy Land. We can safely assume, therefore, that the Jews always recited this blessing, each individual expressing its concepts in his own words. Later, when David and Solomon built the Temple, they formulated a standard text.

A more difficult problem arises with the fourth blessing. There is no dispute in the Talmud with regard to its origins; our Sages instituted it to thank God for His kindness to "the fallen of Beitar." After the destruction of the Second Temple, the Romans besieged a mountain fortress called Beitar. After a long and grueling siege, the Romans finally broke through and slaughtered all the Jews. Then with vicious and gratuitous cruelty, they refused to allow the corpses a decent burial. Miraculously, the corpses did not decompose and were eventually brought to their final rest. In recognition of God's goodness (*hatov*) in preserving the corpses and His benevolence in allowing them to be buried (*hameitiv*), the Sages of Yavneh instituted the fourth blessing. There is, however, an opinion in the Talmud that the fourth blessing is a Biblical requirement. How can this be? Unlike the building of the Temple, there was no precedent or prior concept that foreshadowed the tragic events at Beitar. How then could the blessing have existed from Biblical times?

Let us take a closer look at the themes of each of the four blessings.

The first blessing praises God (*shevach*) for His kindness in providing sustenance for all mankind. The second expresses our gratitude to God (*hodaah*) for the land, the Exodus from Egypt, the covenant of circumcision and the receipt of the Torah. The third, which mentions the Temple, is a prayer (*bakashah*) petitioning God for compassion, for the city of Jerusalem and the Davidic dynasty, for the Temple and for our daily sustenance. The conclusion of the third blessing beseeches God to rebuild Jerusalem (undoubtedly a Rabbinic emendation after the destruction of the Temple).

The fourth blessing introduces an element missing from the first three. In it, we bless God for His continual providence throughout history. There is no specific reference to "the fallen of Beitar." Its message reassures the Jewish people in all unfortunate times that might lead to despair. According to the opinion that this blessing is a Biblical requirement, the Torah did not formulate a precise text from the nation's beginning in the desert. Rather, the Torah left it to the discretion of the Sages to introduce it at a time of great national need. Our Sages chose the time they considered the nadir of Jewish history. The Romans had destroyed Jerusalem and the Temple, slaughtered millions of Jews and driven the survivors into exile. And now they had annihilated Beitar, the last Jewish stronghold in Israel, and left the bodies to rot. Things seemed worse than hopeless.

Just then, God showed the people a glimpse of His hidden providence. He kept the bodies from decomposing, and He engineered their burial. This, the Sages decided, was the appropriate time to institute the blessing of providence. Just as God did not in fact forsake the seemingly exposed and neglected corpses, so too would He not remove His providence from the Jewish people throughout their protracted exile. They too would not "decompose." They too would one day meet a good end. It was precisely at that low point in Jewish history that the fourth blessing brought hope and consolation to the people who had witnessed the tragedy of Beitar and to those who would witness and experience suffering in all future generations.

Upon reflection, it seems that there is a parallel between the blessings of the *Birchas HaMazon* and the thrice-daily *Amidah* prayer. The three blessings of *Birchas HaMazon* express praise, gratitude and supplication, in that order. The three sections of the *Amidah* also address these three themes but in a different order. The first part of the *Amidah,* the opening three blessings, speak God's praises, the middle thirteen are supplications, and the final three express gratitude.

The difference in the purpose of the *Birchas HaMazon* and the *Amidah* explains their difference in order. Both begin with praise, which is, as the Talmud (*Berachos* 34a) explains, the proper salutation when speaking to the King. The *Amidah,* whose essential theme is petition, immediately moves into supplication, and it concludes with expressions of gratitude. Because *Birchas HaMazon,* in contrast, is essentially a statement of gratitude, it moves into the expressions of gratitude and concludes with supplications.

It is customary to remove knives from the table before *Birchas HaMazon.* Why? The Beis Yosef (*Orach Chaim* 120:5) offers a number of reasons, one of which relates to an unfortunate incident recorded in the Jerusalem Talmud. A man, while reciting the third blessing, conjured up lurid images in his mind of the destruction of the Temple and became so distraught that he grabbed a knife lying on the table and stabbed himself. Presumably to prevent a recurrence of this type of episode, the rabbis initiated the custom.

This explanation for the custom is odd, for it seems highly unlikely that a knife on the table would promote the recurrence of such an incident. Millions of Jews for thousands of years had uttered this blessing daily without mishap. No one else had ever come to stab himself until that episode, and with equal probability, no one would seriously consider acting so afterward. Ironically, with the accepted custom, quite the opposite became true. By requiring the removal of knives from the table, we remind ourselves every time we bless God after a meal of the time a man had stabbed himself, and we run the risk that someone slightly unhinged might be tempted to follow suit.

Rather, it would seem that the Sages in their deep wisdom instituted a custom that reminds us of the extent to which we should feel the loss of Jerusalem. As we pray for its restoration, we are reminded that it is possible for someone to feel he cannot live without it, and in so doing, we are inspired to pine earnestly for its restoration.

iii. *Who Owns the Earth?*

WHO OWNS THE EARTH, GOD OR MAN? THE TALMUD (*Berachos* 35a) points out a contradiction in the Psalms. We find in one place (24:1), "The earth and all it contains belong to God." Elsewhere, however, we find (115:16), "The heavens are God's heavens, but He gave the earth to mankind." Which one is it? Does earth still belong to God or did He give it to mankind?

The Talmud resolves this question by making ownership dependent on blessings. Before a person makes a blessing, the bounty of the earth belongs to God. After he makes the blessing, the bounty he seeks becomes his.

This solution is based on the specific commandment to bless God after eating bread (8:10), the only explicit commandment in the entire Torah that calls on us to bless God. The Talmud reasons that if we are required to bless God after having eaten, we must certainly bless Him beforehand as well. Once we make the blessing, the earth's bounty becomes ours.

Upon further reflection, however, some difficulty remains. Let us assume that two people sit down to share a loaf of bread. One makes the blessing, while the other doesn't. How is it possible that the same loaf belongs to the one who made the blessing but with regard to the one who didn't it still belongs to God?

In point of fact, the bounty never ceases to belong to God. Nonetheless, when we make a blessing, expressing our awareness of His benevolence, we become partners in God's creation, so to speak. In acknowledging God, we fulfill our goal in creation. As such, we have usage rights, while the one who makes no blessing does not.

This understanding leads to an important and useful corollary. It is not infrequent to utter a blessing hastily without serious intent, fulfilling our obligation only on a minimal level. We might at that moment feel a pang of regret and resolve to do better next time. In fact, we can still compensate for our shortcoming as long as we are using and enjoying the bounty. The reality is that we continually fulfill the purpose of the blessing in every moment we maintain a hovering awareness that we are partaking of God's benevolence and bounty; by focusing on God's benevolence as long as we are eating, we extend the blessing to envelop the entire meal and transform it into a religious experience. Therefore, even if we made a hasty blessing, we can raise it up to a higher level if we tune in to its true intent at any time during the meal.

iv. Fear of God

CALLING UPON THE PEOPLE TO ADHERE TO A HIGHER STANDARD, Moses declared (10:12), "And now, O Israel, what does God your Lord ask of you? Only to fear God your Lord, to walk in all His ways, to love Him and to serve God your Lord with all your heart and all your soul."

The Talmud (*Berachos* 33b) finds this verse troubling. How can Moses represent these goals to the Jewish people as a small matter when in fact only the most righteous attain constant fear of

God? The Talmud explains that Moses spoke from his own perspective, albeit with Divine inspiration, vis-à-vis the Torah. For Moses, fear of God was a small task.

A question still remains. Why would Moses speak in a form reflecting his own outlook, and generally inapplicable to other people?

Elsewhere (*Menachos* 43b), Rabbi Meir offers a homiletic interpretation, based on a play on words in this verse, that there is an obligation to pronounce one hundred blessings each day. Traditionally, homiletic exegesis is given a lot of latitude (*ein meshivim al hadrush*), but it is still expected to have at least a tenuous conceptual connection to the simple meaning of the verse. In this case, the connection of one hundred blessings to the plain meaning of the text seems far-fetched. Can we find a more substantial connection to the theme of the verse beyond a mere pun?

Rabbinic writings often distinguish two levels of fear and love of God. On a superficial level, our feelings derive from our focus on our own lives. We are afraid that God may punish us, that He may penalize our health, property and perhaps even our very lives. On the other hand, our love for God derives from a sense of gratitude for His benevolence, for the positive impact He makes on our lives. At this level, our blessings heighten our awareness of God's role within the narrow parameters of our lives.

On a more profound level, our own primacy recedes, and we respond to God with rapture and awe regardless of how we are personally affected by His actions. Our importance recedes as we are awed and dwarfed by His infinite majesty, and at the same time, we are irresistibly drawn toward Him. This is a much higher form of fear and love. On this level, our blessings focus on God as benefactor rather than on us as beneficiaries.

According to Rabbi Meir's interpretation of the verse, we can understand how Moses' advice was applicable to the people. According to Rabbi Meir, hidden in Moses' exhortation to the Jewish people was a means to gain fear of God that works on two levels. By increasing the awareness of God's benevolence, as represented by the daily complement of one hundred blessings, one may ultimately gain the sublime level of love and fear of God that Moses experienced. In the interim, by focusing on the benefits from God one stands to lose, the requisite lower level of fear was indeed in the people's grasp.

v. *The Wrong Drummer*

DATHAN AND ABIRAM SEEM TO HAVE BEEN LEFT HOLDING the bag. In the second year of the Jewish sojourn in the desert, Korach tried to wrest the leadership position from Moses and Aaron, his fellow Levites. Dathan and Abiram of the tribe of Reuven were among the adherents to Korach's rebellion. Now, as Moses delivers his valedictory address to the people at the end of his life, he reminds them of various aspects of God's guidance over the previous forty years, including that ill-fated rebellion (11:6), "[And you shall know] what He did to Dathan and Abiram, the sons of Eliav, the son of Reuven, when the earth opened its mouth wide and swallowed them and their households and their tents, and all their wealth at their feet in the midst of all Israel." Moses conspicuously omits to mention Korach, the instigator of the evil. Instead, he focuses only on Dathan and Abiram who were no more than followers. Why is this so?

In actuality, although Korach's sin was far greater than theirs, in one sense it was more explicable. Korach was out for his own gain; a lust for importance and power drove him almost irresistibly. But Dathan and Abiram really did not stand to gain anything in the rebellion; they impulsively joined a fight that was not theirs. Hence Moses again traces the lineage of Dathan and Abiram to Reuven, whom Jacob had characterized as impulsive, "turbulent like water (*pachaz kamayim*)."

Accordingly, we can understand why Moses only mentions Dathan and Abiram but not Korach. In this section, Moses stresses the importance of trusting God and following His guidance, as we see in the prior verses where Moses reminds the people of God's hand in the Exodus and His protection in the desert. In this context, Moses mentions the fate of Dathan and Abiram as an illustration of the consequences of marching to the beat of the wrong drummer.

Altogether, the Torah mentions the fate of Dathan and Abiram three times — in the initial account of Korach's rebellion, when Moses counts the tribe of Reuven and in his valedictory admonition to the Jewish people. Curiously, during the census of Reuven, the Torah lets us know that Dathan and Abiram perished while Korach's sons survived (*Numbers* 26:11). This fact, however, is not mentioned at all in the initial account of Korach's death. Why does the Torah choose this particular time to introduce the fate of Korach's sons?

Perhaps it is because their fate bore a greater philosophical similarity to that of Dathan and Abiram than to that of their own father. Dathan and Abiram stand out as impulsive troublemakers always scrapping to join a fight, people who stood to gain nothing even if Korach succeeded. Korach's sons were the diametric opposites. They stood to gain everything in Korach's rebellion. If Korach had successfully usurped Moses' leadership position he would most likely have established his own dynasty and passed the office down to his heirs. But the response of Korach's sons bespeaks their integrity. They turned away from the rebellion even though they stood to gain power and privilege by it. Therefore, it is when the Torah highlights the shortcomings of Dathan and Abiram that it reveals to us previously undisclosed information about the fate of Korach's sons. Their character stands out in sharp relief.

vi. Check Your Mezuzah

THE TORAH COMMANDS US TO AFFIX THE FIRST TWO PARAgraphs of the *Shema* to our homes (11:20), "And you shall write them on the doorposts of your house and on your gates." The obligation of the homeowner extends beyond the time when he initially affixes the *mezuzah* to his door. According to the law, one must check each *mezuzah* twice every seven years to ascertain that it is still kosher, since even a break in the side of a single letter renders the *mezuzah* invalid.

Our Sages chose a rather imprecise way of expressing the frequency with which a *mezuzah* must be checked — twice in seven years. Why didn't they use more precise measures such as every three and a half years?

Perhaps our Sages sought to connect the *mezuzah* subtly in the minds of the people with another phenomenon in Jewish life cycle that occurs twice in seven years. The Torah requires every landowner to give a supplementary tithe of his produce to paupers (*maaser ani*) during the third and sixth years of the seven-year *Shemittah* cycle in Israel, over and above the standard annual tithe to the Levites. This identical and unusual frequency suggests a connection between the *mezuzah* and the legal institution of alms to the poor.

A pauper is defined as a person without possessions. Most notably, he lacks his own home, the ultimate material possession. A home provides refuge from nature's harsh elements; it also provides security and privacy. The pauper stands in sharp contrast to the homeowner.

By expressing the mandated frequency for checking the *mezuzah* in terms that correspond to the cycle of giving tithes to the pauper, our Sages gave us a veiled reminder that our physical possessions, most prominent of which are our homes, are a gift from God; we could just as easily have been the pauper on the other side of the door. Subtly, our Sages warn us that if we do not use our material blessings to benefit others we might actually lose them. These are the concepts expressed in the second paragraph of the *Shema* that is part of the *mezuzah*.

The question remains: Why did our Sages convey this association with such oblique subtlety? Why not state explicitly that we must check the *mezuzah* as frequently as we give tithes to the pauper?

Our Sages state that the *mezuzah* stands guard over the home. Ignorant people can easily mistake the *mezuzah* for a kind of magical amulet with powerful protective powers. The Rambam decries such a view (*Laws of Mezuzah* 6:13), "Any time a person enters or exits he encounters this expression of God's oneness as reflected by His Name. Recalling [God's] love, he awakens from his befuddled preoccupation with trivial pursuits. Then he realizes that nothing is everlasting except the Creator of the universe, and he immediately returns to the proper path in life."

This is the true message our Sages wanted to convey by creating the linkage between the *mezuzah* and tithes for the poor. Nonetheless, they were concerned that some people might view the *mezuzah* itself as a device that protects against poverty. Therefore, our Sages subtly made this connection discernible only by effort and thought. Someone thoughtful enough to penetrate to their intent would be unlikely to make an ignorant mistake.

פרשת ראה
Parashas Re'eh

i. Textual Nuances

CLOSE READINGS OF THE TEXT OF THE TORAH ALMOST invariably bring to light innumerable textual nuances that might otherwise have been missed. Sometimes they reveal profound concepts or important information, while at other times they simply help us see the incredible precision of the Author's Divine pen. The following is one example.

In the English language, both the second person singular and the second person plural are expressed by the word "you." Most other languages differentiate between the two. In Hebrew, *atah* expresses the singular "you" and *atem* the plural "you."

Twice in one chapter, the Torah speaks about our obligation to rejoice with our children in Jerusalem, yet there is an important difference in the use of the second person pronoun. In the first mention, God commands (12:11-12), "That is where you shall bring all that I command you, your burnt offerings and your feast offerings . . . And you shall rejoice before God your Lord, you (*atem*), your sons (*beneichem*), your daughters (*benoseichem*) . . ."

The use of the second person plural indicates that God is speaking to the collective rather than the individual.

A few verses later, God commands (12:17-18), "You shall not be allowed to eat the tithe of your grain and your wine . . . You shall eat them before God your Lord in the place God your Lord will choose, you (*atah*), your son (*bincha*), your daughter (*bitecha*) . . . and you shall rejoice before God." Here the Torah switches to the second person singular.

Upon reflection, we can discover a basis for this distinction. The first verse discusses the obligation to bring festival sacrifices, something incumbent on all Jews. Fittingly, the Torah uses the collective second person plural. The second verse obliges farmers and vintners to bring a portion of their grain and wines to Jerusalem. This directive applies only to people engaged in agriculture. It does not necessarily apply to the whole of the nation or even to a majority in less agrarian times. Here, the Torah expresses the obligation as an individual rather than a collective one. The Torah precisely reflects this by use of the second person singular.

ii. Blood and Children

AMONG THE ENUMERATED FORBIDDEN FOODS, THE TORAH proscribes the lifeblood of an animal with unusual emphasis (12:23-25). "Only be strong not to eat the blood, for the blood is the life, and you shall not eat the life with the meat. Do not eat it, pour it onto the ground like water. Do not eat it in order that He will be good to you and your children after you, for you will have done what is right in the eyes of God."

Each of God's commandments is, of course, the multidimensional product of His unfathomable infinite wisdom, and when the reasons are presented in the Torah we are afforded a mere glimpse of its essence. Here, somewhat unusually, the Torah goes to great lengths to explain the reasons and benefits of observance. Why is this so?

We may also note that the Torah here makes special mention of the benefit to our children. Why would specifically refraining from eating animal blood benefit our children more so than other proscribed foods for which no such promise is made? Furthermore, why does the Torah use the unusual expression "your children after you"? Isn't it self-explanatory that children come after their parents? What additional meaning do these words convey?

To answer those questions, let us for a moment consider a child's normal development. The Torah (*Genesis* 8:21) states, "The inclination of man is evil from his youth (*ne'urav*)." Our Sages understand this to mean that the inclination for evil is present from the moment the fetus struggles (*nin'ar*) to escape its cramped confines (youth and struggle share a common etymological root, *naar*, נַעַר). The evil inclination (*yetzer hara*) is a descriptive term which reflects the capacity of man to resist the development of ever closer levels of awareness in relationship to God. It stems from the animal side of man (*nefesh habahamis*) with its earthly desires, and it creates barriers between man and God.

An important aspect of a child's upbringing is to help him gain control over the instinctual side of the human personality that is present from conception. A child does not reach legal maturity until his intellectual faculties are strong enough to control his impulses. Until then, it is the parent's responsibility to guide him in this direction.

Another facet of children is that they identify with their parents and are deeply influenced by their parents' example. For instance, parents with outstanding virtues of kindness will tend to have kind children, while parents who lecture about kindness will have children who also lecture about kindness.

In this context, we can gain a new dimension of insight into the Torah's injunction against consumption of animal blood. Man experiences, on a conscious and unconscious level, that to a certain extent he is what he eats. Specifically in the prohibition against consumption of the "animal," the Torah informs us that our restraint will benefit our impressionable charges, whose task as youths is to master their instinctual (*nefesh habahamis*) nature. When we reject our animalistic nature by "spilling the blood like water," we set an example for our children who come "after us." In this way, the observance of the commandment is good for us and for them.

Upon consideration, we may discover another deeper though subtle way our observance of this commandment benefits our children.

In *Parashas Mishpatim* (*Exodus* 21:15-17), we noted that the juxtaposition of the laws of kidnaping and abusing parents alludes to the inclination of parents to seek to rectify their own mistakes or fulfill their unmet longings vicariously through their children. Thus, when parents "kidnap" their offspring in this way, a resentful child who hits or curses may emerge. This kidnaping may take the form of wanting a child to be a good baseball player or, for others, a righteous scholar. When this desire is driven by the parents' own unrequited personal longings, it will frequently harm the child. In these circumstances, the impulse to fix the child flows from a person's own weakness. He finds it easier to fix his deficits in his child than to improve himself.

There is also another area where a person can attempt to get a "quick fix." At a deep, unconscious level, man senses that he is what he eats. An animal may represent certain traits or circumstances a person desires, such as strength, power, freedom, courage. In allowing us to eat animals, the Torah forbids us to consume that part which reflects the animal's essence. The pagan religions intuitively understood the power of these unconscious forces in man, and they are replete with totem animal meals.

Theoretically, there are two ways a person may incorrectly try to fill some need or lacking he senses in himself. He may project himself onto another (projective identification) and fix that person (i.e., his child), or he may try to incorporate (literally ingest) something external into himself. The Torah's approach to resolving one's shortcomings is by introspection, prayer and courageous acts of free-will. The verse teaches that if a person refrains from correcting himself in the primitive way of eating the animal's lifeblood, he may merit not to try to correct himself through his children as well. In this circumstance, his refraining from the blood will be good for him and his children, as the Torah so states.

iii. Dead Men's Gods

FULL VICTORY OVER THE CANAANITES WILL NOT COME, Moses tells the people, when they defeat the defending armies on the battlefield. The ultimate battle will not be fought until afterward (12:30-31). "Watch yourself lest you become drawn to them after they have been destroyed before you, and lest you seek out their gods, saying, 'How did these nations worship their gods? I, too, will do the same.' You shall not do so to God your Lord, for everything that is an abomination to God, that He hates, they have done for their gods; for they have even burned their sons and daughters in the fire for their gods."

These verses reveal the great seductive power of idolatry. Consider the situation. The Jewish people have just conquered the land. With God's help, they have destroyed the indigenous defenders and completely exposed the impotence of their gods. God's power is manifest; the pagan's imaginary deities are discredited. Incredibly, at this moment of Jewish triumph, the Torah warns the victors not to be drawn to the gods of the vanquished. Why would they be drawn to these dead men's gods or find their cults attractive? What is at the root of this strange seductive power?

In actuality, idolatry is much more apt to arise out of the psychological needs of idol worshipers than from an intellectual mistake. Idolatry allows its adherents to create and observe, in the guise of a religion, a system of rituals and practices that satisfy their primitive urges and address their insecurities. Even when these pagan religions call upon their adherents to make sacrifices, there is a simultaneous satisfaction of deep primitive urges. Often this attraction is so subtle that the worshipers, unaccustomed to self-examination, are unaware of its insidious nature.

The Jewish people entering the Holy Land, although victorious on the battlefield, would not be immune to the drives and character flaws that draw people to idolatry. It was quite possible that they would turn in that direction as they contended with the psychological pressures of their daily lives. However, having no direct experience with idolatrous cults, they might be intrigued by the vestiges of the destroyed cults all around them, sensing their psychological appeal. And they would ask, "How did these nations worship their gods? I, too, will do the same." The Torah forbids them to do this and warns them (12:31) that, in the end, such practices can even lead their followers to throw their children into the fire.

Ironically, the practice of child immolation, from a psychological perspective, reflects selfishness rather than altruistically intended, though misguided, religious fervor. The practitioners may tell themselves they are sacrificing their beloved children selflessly, but the exact opposite is true. These supposedly religious people are tremendously narcissistic, full of undeflected self-love. Attached to the physical reality and fearful of their own mortality, they are prepared to make the penultimate sacrifice of a relatively expendable part of themselves, namely their children, in order to protect that which is most important, namely themselves.

iv. *Knowing the Unknowable*

CLOVEN HOOVES AND CUD CHEWING ARE THE TWO SIGNS OF a kosher animal; an animal missing one or both of these signs is deemed nonkosher. Innumerable animals lack both kosher signs, but the Torah specifies (14:7) only four species that lack only one — the camel, rabbit and hyrax, which chew their cud but have no cloven hooves, and the swine, which has cloven hooves but does not chew its cud.

The Torah recorded this curious fact 3,300 years ago. Now, centuries and millennia later, science has identified more than five thousand animal species, and still, these four remain the only species that have one kosher sign but lack the other. Indeed, the Talmud (*Chullin* 60b) declares that this proves the Divine origin of the Torah.

Perhaps we can identify yet another example of clairvoyance in this *parashah*, which offers additional proof.

In the ancient world, as the knowledge of Judaism spread, most intelligent pagans came to recognize it as the one true religion, although they were reluctant to convert because of the demands of Jewish practice. Around that time, Christianity appeared, sporting Jewish values and morality and initially a somewhat similar theology but discarding Jewish practice. Not surprisingly, Christianity achieved great success and popularity, and even today, it still dominates the Western world.

Had the early Christians launched a totally new religion, it would most probably have fallen by the wayside. Instead, it claimed authenticity by piggybacking on the truth and credibility of the Torah. But basing itself on Judaism presented a problem. How could they explain away all practices and obligations so clearly spelled out in the Torah? The response of the early Church was to claim they were no longer required. The Nazarene had fulfilled the Torah's precepts, and all that is now necessary to gain eternity is to have faith in him.

The Torah anticipated the appearance of false prophets over the ages (13:2), "Should there arise among you a false prophet or a dreamer of dreams . . . do not heed the words of that prophet . . ."

Now let us look at the verse immediately preceding the laws of the false prophet (13:1). "Everything I command you, safeguard and do, do not add to it nor detract from it."

Christianity understood that it needed to base itself on the ancient and uncontested Torah of the Jews. The Torah, however, makes it clear that any movement that tinkers with Jewish practice is illegitimate.

v. *The Thrift-Shop Option*

MEAT FROM AN ANIMAL THAT WAS NOT RITUALLY SLAUGHtered is not kosher. What should be done with it? The Torah's answer is subject to interpretation (14:21). "You shall not eat any carcass (*neveilah*), you shall give it to the stranger (*ger*) in your citadels so that he may eat it, or sell it to a gentile (*nachri*), for you are a holy people to God your Lord."

The "stranger (*ger*)" to whom one should give it is an alien resident, known as a *ger toshav,* who undertakes to keep the Seven Noahide Laws.[1] He may eat nonkosher meat, since the prohibition is not a Noahide law. These then are the two potential recipients — an alien resident and a gentile.

The Torah seems to make a distinction between the two. We may give nonkosher meat to an alien resident or sell it to a gentile. Can it be done in the reverse as well? The Talmud (*Pesachim* 21b) presents two conflicting views on this question. Rabbi Yehudah insists that it must be done exactly as written (*devarim kich'savam*). We may not sell the meat to an alien resident nor give it to a gentile. Rabbi Meir connects both transactions with both recipients; he reads the verse as "you shall give it to the stranger (*ger*) in your citadels so that he may eat it or sell it," and at the same time as, "you shall give it so that he may eat it or sell it to a gentile (*nachri*)."

Each of these views raises difficulties of its own.

---

1. These laws include prohibitions against idolatry, murder, theft, adultery and eating flesh from a living animal, and a requirement to establish courts of law.

According to Rabbi Meir, why does the Torah instruct us in such an obfuscated manner? Why couldn't the verse state simply that the meat may be "given or sold to a stranger or a gentile"?

According to Rabbi Yehudah, the right to give the meat to a resident alien seems superfluous. Once the Torah allows us to profit from the sale of *neveilah* (nonkosher) meat, why would anyone ever give it away to a *ger*? Furthermore, if the sale of *neveilah* meat is permitted, and if the *ger* is permitted to eat it, why indeed is it forbidden to sell him the meat?

In the Jewish scheme of things, nonkosher meat is an object that has lost its value, like old, worn-out garments. Some use can still be squeezed out of them, but they are basically discards. Essentially, an animal is used either for work or for slaughter as food. However, if an animal dies without being ritually slaughtered, it no longer serves any of these functions; it becomes a discard.

What do we do with worn-out garments ready to be discarded? We may give them to friends or to charity. Or else, we may sell them to a thrift shop or run a garage sale. However, although there exists the possibility of converting the clothing to a little cash, no one would ever dream of selling them to a friend. It would be an insult to take money from a friend for an essentially valueless item.

This then is Rabbi Yehudah's logic. Nonkosher meat, to a Jew, is essentially valueless. The proper thing would be to give it to the resident *ger*, since we have an obligation to support him. It would be offensive and unconscionable to sell a mostly worthless, perishable discard to him. Furthermore, it would make him feel rejected from the Jewish community.

Still, if the carcass had some market value, the Torah allows the owner to recover it, like selling old clothes to a thrift shop. He may sell it to a gentile. He may not, however, give it to a gentile gratis, for if so, he might as well have given it to a *ger*, just as it would be improper to give the old clothes to a thrift shop when he could just as easily have given them to his nearby family member or friend.

Perhaps Rabbi Meir also subscribed to this logic, but he did not construe the verses of the Torah as an actual codification of these protocols into law. Thus, in order to convey the ethical priorities, the Torah presented the law in this cumbersome manner that allows all options but implies a preference.

vi. *Abstract Apples*

FOUR YEARS OUT OF THE SEVEN-YEAR *SHEMITTAH* CYCLE, the Torah requires Jewish landowners living in Israel during the Temple eras to allocate a supplementary harvest tithe called *maaser sheni*. This sanctified tithe was not meant to be given away. Rather, the Torah obligated its owner to eat it and share it with family and friends — but only in Jerusalem. But what if it was inconvenient or impractical to bring one's perishables all the way to Jerusalem? The Torah addresses this issue (14:24-25). "And if the distance will be too great for you, so that you cannot carry it, for the place is too far from you . . . then you may exchange it for money; wrap up the money in your hand, and go to the place that God your Lord will choose."

Since the landowner cannot bring the food to Jerusalem, the Torah allows him to redeem it temporarily for money. This procedure transfers the sanctity of the food to the redemption money, which the landowner brings, "wrapped up to go," to Jerusalem. Once he arrives in Jerusalem, he purchases food with the sanctified money, thereby transferring the sanctity to the new food.

The word the Torah uses for "wrap up," *tzarta*, is cognate with the word for "image" or "form," *tzurah*. This a peculiar way to express the temporary exchange of the food for money. From this, the Talmud (*Bava Metzia* 54a) deduces that one may exchange the original harvest food for a minted coin that has an image or words imprinted on it and not a smooth silver unminted disc. What is the concept behind this law? Why does the Torah insist that only minted coins be used?

Money is a curious economic phenomenon. While initially currency was valued by its weight in precious or semiprecious metals, it eventually metamorphosed to the point where it was no longer a commodity. Its value was no longer based on its utility or even the potential use of the precious metals it contained to manufacture ornaments. Its value derived from an abstract concept reflecting its acceptance as coin of the realm. Money became a repository of value rather than an object of intrinsic value. This concept is especially manifest in our own times when most nations use fiat paper money, which is not even backed by gold reserves. A smooth silver disc is a commodity, a nugget of precious metal. A minted coin is money.

In this light, we can distinguish between transactions of barter and money. Barter exchanges one useful item for another in a fair exchange, depending in general on the two parties to the transaction having differing needs; for instance, one needs a bicycle while the other needs a microwave oven. As opposed to this, the use of money and, more generally, currency is an abstract method for extracting an item's value in a theoretical yet practical way.

To make this clearer, let us consider two ways to turn apples into bread. One, we can barter a bag of apples for a loaf of bread. Two, we can sell apples and use the money to buy bread. In the first, barter completely obliterates the identity of apples during the exchange. When we sell the apples for money, however, we have not replaced them with another commodity that has its own identity that overrides the identity of the apples. Rather, we have stored the value of the apples in the money. We now have abstract apples.

By requiring the *maaser sheni* tithes to be exchanged for a minted coin with a form, the Torah prohibits barter, whereby the intrinsic value of the coin's metal determines its value. The tithes were invested with *kedushah*, holiness, that would not allow them to be swapped for another item, even for the purpose of facilitating their transport to Jerusalem where it would be bartered back into food. The only leniency of the Torah is to extract the value of the food and reconstitute it in Jerusalem. To exchange food through barter desecrates its holiness; it is as if we are equating this food with its loftier goal to the exchanged metal. Only currency, coins that have images, may be used for redemption. The Torah reveals this concept beautifully and concisely in a single word, *tzarta*.

vii. One Path to Unity

THE TORAH IS VERY SPECIFIC ABOUT THE VENUE OF THE Passover sacrifice (16:5-6). "You shall not be allowed to slaughter the paschal offering in one of your citadels that God your Lord gives you; rather, at the place where God your Lord will choose to rest His Name, there shall you slaughter the paschal offering."

A word in this verse stands out as seemingly superfluous, the prohibition to slaughter the paschal lamb in "one" of your citadels. Wouldn't it have been sufficient to forbid slaughtering the lamb in "your citadels"? The Talmud (*Zevachim* 114b; *Pesachim* 79b, 91a) notes this anomaly and offers a number of solutions.

A question still remains. Why does the Torah insert the seemingly superfluous word "one" with regard to the festival of Passover and not with regard to the other festivals, which also feature sacrificial offerings that must be brought to the Temple in Jerusalem?

Perhaps we can find an additional thought in this verse according to the simple meaning of the text. One of the underlying themes of Passover is the birth and unity of the Jewish people, which expresses itself in numerous laws and customs of the Passover service. In order to include everyone in the Passover sacrifice, the Torah provides an additional day, one month later, for those unable to participate in the sacrifice on its designated date. One of the most famous lines of the Passover Haggadah is the statement of embrace, "All who are needy, let them come in and eat." On a symbolic level, the Maharal discerns the concept of unity in the law that the paschal lamb must be roasted, not cooked. Roasting, he explains, causes meat to contract and come closer together, while cooking causes it to expand and loosen. Finally, although many sacrificial lambs were brought, the Torah expresses the requirement in the singular, "they shall slaughter it," as if to suggest that one animal for the whole nation would be preferable.

In this light, perhaps we can gain new insight into the Torah's prohibition against slaughtering the paschal lamb in "one of your citadels." There may come a time when people will think that the concept of Jewish unity can be expressed in venues other than Jerusalem. They may make unity an end in itself and forget that it is but a means to achieve perfect fulfillment of our covenant with God. They may remove the concept of unity from Jerusalem, the seat of the Divine Presence, and transfer it to "one of your citadels" — unity without religion.

Sadly, this has happened again and again throughout our checkered history, from the Sadducees and Hellenists of antiquity to the secular Zionists of the recent past. These groups sought to find a different focus for Jewish unity, and they have consistently failed. Jewish unity, as the language of the verse suggests, goes hand in hand with unequivocal commitment to God.

viii. *Horses and Servants*

HOW MUCH SUPPORT ARE WE SUPPOSED TO GIVE THE INDIgent? The Torah provides the answer (15:7-8). "Do not harden your heart or close your hand against your destitute brother. Rather, you shall surely open your hand to him and you shall support him, enough for his lack that he is lacking."

"Enough for his lack that he is lacking." What does this mean? What is the significance of the redundancy? The Talmud (*Kesubos* 67b) derives two guidelines from this phrase. "Enough for his lack" tells us that we are not obliged to make the poor man wealthy. "That he is lacking" tells us that we are obliged to provide him with horses and servants if he was accustomed to having them before he became impoverished.

According to this interpretation, there seems to be an internal contradiction in the verse itself. On the one hand, the verse tells us that we are not obliged to make the pauper wealthy. At the same time, it tells us to restore the rich man to the lap of luxury. Wouldn't that be considered making him wealthy? Furthermore, isn't the Torah demanding a great deal by requiring even men of modest means to contribute toward the restoration of the once-rich pauper to a standard of living far above their own?

Because the Torah overflows with compassion and love for the poor, defenseless and unfortunate, there is a tendency among some to view Judaism as a socialist doctrine, opposing the unequal distribution of wealth and seeking to eliminate supposed inequities.

This is simply not true. According to the Torah, wealth and poverty are assigned by God, not by man. Moreover, the last of the Ten Commandments states specifically, "You shall not covet" what another person has; socialism covets. The Torah is indeed in favor of equality but in the spiritual rather than the material sense. Each person is afforded an equal opportunity to develop an ever closer relationship with God through the challenges of his own unique life.

Later on, the Torah again seems to be addressing the potential for tension among the economic classes (23:26). "When you come into the standing grain of your fellow, you may pluck ripe ears with your hand, but you may not lift a sickle against the standing grain of your fellow." The Torah permits the agricultural worker to pluck raw grain with his hands and take it home, but it denies him the efficiency of a sickle.

Here again, we find an apparent redundancy in the verse. The Torah originally tells us that the discussion applies to a laborer coming into the standing grain "of your fellow." Why then is it necessary to repeat that he should not take a sickle to the standing grain "of your fellow"?

Perhaps the Torah here hints at a possible motivation of the laborer. Certainly, he wants the grain in order to feed his family. But it is also natural and common for a laborer to resent the landowner who enjoys greater economic benefit from his sweat and toil than he himself does. This was the rage that fueled Marxism. From this perspective, the laborer may be more intent on the perceived injustice than on his personal need. The Torah appears to anticipate such an attitude. Translated literally, the concluding phrase reads, "Do not take a sickle to the standing of your fellow." Envy can propel the laborer to mow down the grain and, at an unconscious level reflecting his aggression toward his privileged boss, to seek to mow down the landowner himself. The redundant "fellow" (*rei'echa*) reminds us that he is our fellow and friend whose situation the Torah elsewhere forbids us to covet. He has the portion God bestowed on him, and the laborer may not act out his envy and aggression toward it with a sickle.

With this understanding, we can perhaps better explain the obligation to restore the impoverished person to the lap of luxury, if that is what he once enjoyed. Each person has his own special challenges that God's providence has set for him. Some struggle in poverty, others contend with wealth. Both of these pose spiritual challenges, although different from each other, and it is incumbent on each of us to focus on the challenges God has set for him.

The impoverished wealthy man is not a true pauper. He is a wealthy man in pauper's clothes. His former circumstances were of the wealthy sort, from which he has fallen, perhaps because he did not deal well with its challenges. When we restore him to his former position, it is not we who make him rich. We merely enable him to continue the singular struggle God has set for him. We should not begrudge him his task; it comes with its own set of difficulties and struggles, among which is proper consideration and concern for those lacking in material wealth. Rather, we should focus on achieving spiritual success right where we find ourselves.

ix. *The Second Gift Is Better*

CIRCUMSTANCES MAY SOMETIMES FORCE A JEW TO INDENture to another Jew. Should this happen, the Torah teaches us to treat him with respect and dignity. Furthermore, the Torah ensures that he return to civilian life with the wherewithal to make a fresh start (15:13-14). "And when you set him free from yourself, do not send him away empty-handed. You shall surely give him gifts (*haanek taanik lo*), you shall give him from your flocks, granaries and vineyards with which God has blessed you."

The words "you shall surely give him gifts," expressed in the Hebrew as *haanek taanik*, translate literally as "give you shall give." What is the significance of the double mention of gifting?

The Midrash (*Sifrei* 120) explains that we are supposed to emulate God, who gave wealth to the Jewish people in Egypt and then again on the shores of the Sea of Reeds. We, too, must bestow gifts on our indentured servants who go free, and then bestow gifts on them a second time.

Why is it necessary to give two gifts? Wouldn't it be as effective to give a single larger gift?

The answer lies in the psychology of the recipient. An indentured servant going free understands that his former master has a certain obligation to him and is therefore giving him a gift. He is appreciative but not overwhelmed. When he receives the second gift, however, his sense of self-worth greatly expands. Since the master has fulfilled his obligation with the first gift, the servant sees the second gift as a spontaneous expression of esteem and appreciation. Reciprocally, his dignity and self-esteem are more fully restored. This is what the master should strive to accomplish for his former servant. Of course, once the second gift becomes obligatory it loses some of this ego-boosting capacity. Nonetheless, it retains some in the way the law is formulated and our coming to so understand it.

x. *Who's in the Citadel?*

UNLIKE THE SECULAR CALENDAR WHICH IS A HAPHAZARD amalgamation of unrelated celebrations and observances, the Jewish calendar charts the cyclical progression of the relationship between God and the Jewish people through the year. Each festival, celebration and observance builds on the ones that preceded it and sets the stage for the ones that will follow.

Starting with Passover, which celebrates the Exodus from Egypt and the establishment of our relationship with God, the calendar moves on to Shavuos, which celebrates the receiving of the Torah and its instructions. Succos, the final festival, celebrates

God's benevolent providence. The second half of the year features the rabbinic festivals of Chanukah and Purim, described by the *Zohar* as *is'arusa di'le'satta* (the awakening from below), in which we became more active participants in forging our bond with God.

A closer look at the Torah's description of the festivals reveals one manifestation of the dynamic progression of the Jewish calendar. All festivals are to be celebrated with joyous meals. They are times to be shared with those less fortunate than ourselves, times to achieve new dimensions in spirituality, times to focus on the exaltation of the soul rather than the exclusive gratification of the body. The Rambam writes that one who fails to share his holiday meal with the needy has not fulfilled his obligation; he has only fed his belly. This applies to all the meals of all the festivals. Nonetheless, there are subtle differences in the way the Torah presents this obligation.

Let us first examine the reference to Passover (16:7). "You shall roast [the lamb] and eat it in the place God your Lord chooses." Although we derive elsewhere by exegesis that we must share every festival meal with the needy, the Torah does not mention it explicitly with respect to Passover.

The first specific mention occurs with the festival of Shavuos (16:10-11). "Then you shall observe the festival of Shavuos . . . You shall rejoice before God your Lord, you, your son, your daughter, your servants, your maidservant, the Levite who is in your citadels, the proselyte, the orphan and the widow who are among you." Notice that sons, daughters, servants, maidservants and Levites are considered "in your citadels," while proselytes, orphans and widows are only considered "among you."

Finally, we see a shift in the presentation of the festival of Succos (16:13-14). "You shall make the festival of Succos . . . You shall rejoice on your festival, you, your son, your daughter, your servant, your maidservant, the Levite, the proselyte, the orphan and the widow who are in your citadels." Everyone is now considered "in your citadels," even proselytes, orphans and widows.

We are faced with a number of obvious questions. Why does the Torah make no mention of sharing bounty during the joyous celebration of Passover, since the obligation encompasses it as well? Why are the proselyte, orphan and widow described as being "among you" with regard to Shavuos and "in your citadels" with regard to Succos? Finally, why are the Levites grouped together with children and slaves, who form the nuclear family? Wouldn't it have been more logical to group them with the equally landless proselyte?

Perhaps these differences reflect the dynamics of the Jewish calendar. Let us consider. We celebrate Passover before the harvest is in, and therefore, the Torah makes no explicit mention of joy or sharing. By Shavuos, the harvest is complete but not processed, and the Torah begins to speak openly of joy and sharing. But the joy and confidence are still somewhat hesitant, and the landowners are not quite ready to fling open the gates of their citadels to the disenfranchised. Only the Levite is mentioned as present during this time, because he teaches Torah and should be regarded as a household member. The others remain outside the citadels. They are just "among you."

When Succos arrives and the grain is fully harvested and processed, the bounty and joy are without reservations. Landowners are feeling blessed. It is here that the Torah imposes upon them in their expansive state that they should invite everyone into the citadels to join them. It is with the culminating festival that the joy and the sharing should be complete.

xi. Standing on One Leg

PROSELYTES TO JUDAISM ARE COURAGEOUS PEOPLE, AND the Torah expresses a special concern for these landless people without Jewish relatives. In elaborating the laws of the festival, the Torah repeatedly reminds us to include the proselytes in our celebrations. Cut off from the people of their birth and often not entirely familiar with their new environment, proselytes are vulnerable to feelings of loneliness and alienation, and we are called upon to set them at their ease.

The Talmud (*Shabbos* 31a) relates a story about a gentile who was considering converting to Judaism. He approached Shammai, one of the two leading Sages of that generation, and offered to convert if Shammai would explain the Torah to him while standing on one leg. Shammai drove him away with a builder's rod (*amas habinyan*). The gentile then approached Hillel, the other leading Sage of that generation, with the same request. Hillel agreed and stated, "Do not do to your friend that which is hateful to you. This is the Torah. All the rest is interpretation and elaboration. Go out and learn it." Pleased with this response, the gentile converted.

We may ask, why did the gentile find Hillel's reply so satisfactory? Furthermore, how are we to understand Shammai's harsh response?

Let us first consider the gentile's request. It was actually quite offensive. He had disdainfully assumed that the venerated Sages' accumulated scholarship of a lifetime could be expounded while standing on one foot. It was more an expression of ridicule and disrespect than the sober inquiry of a curious mind.

Hillel, however, did not take offense. His response to this affront was indirect and subtle. Without embarrassing the questioner, Hillel was in effect saying, "You are approaching this conversion from the wrong perspective, as your aggressive and demeaning tone indicates. This sort of hostile attitude is antithetical to the fundamental values of Judaism, which directs us to treat every person with the respect we expect for ourselves."

Subtly, Hillel instructed the gentile about his mistake, and the gentile was so impressed with Hillel's wisdom and sensitivity that he converted.

With this thought, we may better understand Shammai's reply. The Jewish people have a dual nature. On the one hand, we are the chosen people, the "firstborn" nation of God, deserving the respect of the world as His representatives. On the other hand, we are a people deeply aware that our destiny is determined foremost by the merit of our patriarchs. Furthermore, collectively we have a keen grasp of man's insignificance in relation to God, and we are humbled. Thus, the duality of our role requires us to be at the same time dignified and humble, with the pure intention of fulfilling God's will selflessly.

Shammai and his school represented the aspect of the Jewish people that called for respect, while Hillel and his school represented the aspect of humility. They were not in conflict; they complemented each other. When the gentile approached Shammai with his question, the venerable Sage reacted calmly and deliberately with the response appropriate for him. He denounced the disrespect he encountered with a sweep of the builder's rod.[2] Hillel, however, represented the humble side of the Jewish people, and as such, he was more patient with the gentile.[3]

Perhaps we can also say that once the gentile heard Hillel's reply he retroactively understood Shammai's response as well. He realized that these were Sages of comparable stature, and when he saw how Hillel treated him, he intuited that Shammai's response could not have been just a burst of violent emotion. Following that line of reasoning, he arrived at the correct conclusion, that the Jewish people were at once noble and humble and that everything was directed to God. This is what convinced him to convert.

---

2. The word *amas* (rod) may also be pronounced *aimas*, which means fear or awe. Shammai felt that for a Sage such as himself to be indifferent to ridicule diminished the reverence due to God. This may have been his subtle allusion in the choice of the *amas* to drive him out.

3. That two Talmudic schools should represent the duality of the Jewish people has a corollary in recent times. Two great Lithuanian *yeshivos*, Slobodka and Novardok, focused on *mussar* (ethical teachings), but they had radically different styles. Slobodka sought to elevate its students by stressing the greatness of man created in God's image. Students were encouraged to act with utmost dignity. Conversely, the Novardokers felt man's sense of self-importance must be overcome in order to achieve closeness to God. They practiced self-belittlement to this end.

פרשת שופטים
Parashas Shoftim

i. Covering All the Bases

IN ORDER TO MAINTAIN THE INTEGRITY OF THE JUSTICE system, the Torah establishes three rules (16:19), "Do not subvert justice, do not show favoritism, nor shall you accept a bribe, for bribery blinds the eyes of the wise and corrupts the words of the just."

There are three components to every court case — the relevant law, the litigants who vie for advantage before the court and the judge who tries the case. In this one verse, the Torah, in its precise style, covers all the bases by warning against willful tampering with any of the three components.

In the first case, the Torah, in order to safeguard the integrity of the law, anticipates the possibility of a judge who questions the fairness of a commandment and decides to act in what he considers a more equitable manner. For instance, he may consider it unfair for a firstborn to get a double share of inherited property, and consequently, he may divide an estate evenly among all the heirs. Against this self-righteousness, the Torah warns the judge not to "subvert justice" by following his personal inclinations. Irrespective of them, the law must stand sacrosanct.

In the second case, the Torah safeguards the equality of the litigants by proscribing favoritism in any form. If one of the litigants is a respected community activist or a well-known scholar, the judge may be inclined to treat him with the deference due to a person of stature. Conversely, if one of the litigants is an extremely needy or unfortunate person, the judge may speak to him with especial kindness and compassion. Here, the Torah warns the judge not to "show favoritism" and thereby put the other litigant at a disadvantage.

Finally, the Torah demands the complete integrity of the judge by prohibiting payment in any shape or form, even if it is given to encourage him to rule in accordance with the law, or even if he accepts gifts from both sides simultaneously. Accepting payment of any sort, the Torah declares, obfuscates the judge's vision and corrupts his judgment.

Thus, in one concise verse, the Torah addresses and safeguards all three essential components of judicial litigation.

ii. *Stumbling on Stallions*

HORSES WERE VALUABLE IN THE ANCIENT WORLD, AND IT seems that Egypt had them in great abundance. In fact, the Torah restricts Jewish kings from having too many horses, because it would lead to close contact with Egypt (17:15-16). "You shall surely appoint a king over yourselves . . . only (*rak*) he shall not accumulate too many horses for himself, so that he will not return the people to Egypt in order to accumulate horses, for God has said to you, 'You shall not persist (*lo sosifun*) in returning on this road again.'"

The last words of the verse stand as a separate commandment

directed to all Jews rather than to the king alone. "You shall not persist in returning on this road [to Egypt] again." The Torah forbids a Jew to live in the land of Egypt. According to the Rambam, this prohibition applies at all times, regardless of any shifts in the government, culture or ethnicity of the indigenous population.

Why should living in Egypt be forbidden if any or all of these elements have changed? What would connect the new Egypt to the old?

By forever prohibiting a return to Egypt, God has established that the return to that land, and to the ancient culture of which it is an eternal reminder, is a sign of an overall national regression. The Jewish nation was born when God chose to bring us forth to freedom from the iron crucible of Egypt; our *raison d'être* is defined by our eternal allegiance to the will of God. No nation before Egypt had ever so denied the reality of God's presence, nor would any nation afterward ever do so to such an extent. The prohibition against living in Egypt institutionalizes the idea that there is a place and belief to which we can "never go back again."

A question remains with regard to the placement of this universal prohibition. Why does the Torah present it within the context of the commandment forbidding a Jewish king to accumulate too many horses rather than as a separate and direct commandment to all the people?

The word "only" (*rak*, רַק) in the phrase "only [the king] shall not accumulate too many horses for himself" appears as a caveat, a warning to those people who expressed a desire to have a king, saying (17:14), "I will establish over me a king like all the nations that surround me." A king represents a powerful central government, with obvious advantages for efficiency, economy and safety. But, warns the Torah, there is also danger inherent in this form of government. The king may seek to accumulate stables of steeds.

What is the significance of a superabundance of horses? What danger would they pose to the welfare of the Jewish state?

Horses in the ancient world were the ultimate weapon of war. The artillery (war chariots) and the cavalry depended on a reliable supply of powerful steeds. By warning the king not to accumulate too many horses, the Torah in effect warns him not to build an excessively large army, since doing so would draw the Jewish nation back toward Egypt and all that it represents.

The Egyptians witnessed the greatest revelation of God's mastery of the world, and yet, they remained defiant. Living in splendid isolation with the inexhaustible supply of Nile River water, the Egyptians became intoxicated with their own self-sufficiency; they could not concede to a Higher Power. A powerful standing army could have the same effect on the Jewish nation, giving rise to the illusion that security lay within their own power. While the Jewish people are meant to make reasonable efforts to protect themselves, they must never forget that true security lies in the God's hands. As Moses warned (8:11;17), "Beware lest you forget God your Lord . . . and you say in your heart, 'My power and the strength of my hand has brought me this triumph.'" An overemphasis on military preparedness can lead us down this path. Thus, the Torah simultaneously enjoins the king from seeking excessive security and also prohibits all Jewish people to return to live in Egypt.

The language at the end of the verse, "You shall not persist (*lo sosifun*) in returning on this road again," resonates with the language of redemption Moses used when he spoke to Pharaoh (*Exodus* 10:29), "You have spoken correctly, I shall not persist (*lo osif*) to see your face again." Thus, the language of the prohibition against living in Egypt reminds us of the Exodus and the special destiny that arose from it.

iii. Land Grabs Are Doubly Deplorable

REAL ESTATE CANNOT BE LIFTED UP AND CARRIED AWAY, BUT it can nonetheless be stolen. The Torah forbids the surreptitious moving of boundary markers (19:14).

"You shall not encroach on your neighbor's boundary that the predecessors set, in your inheritance to which you shall accede, in the land that God your Lord gives you to possess it."

Rashi points out that this prohibition is redundant, since the Torah has already forbidden robbery of any kind. The verse's purpose, Rashi cryptically explains, is to cause one who violates it to transgress two prohibitions.

One may wonder: What purpose is there in adding a second prohibition to that which is already forbidden?

We must conclude that the two prohibitions address different aspects of the same forbidden deed. The general prohibition against robbery addresses the inviolability of property rights; it is forbidden to take that which belongs to another. The specific prohibition against land larceny, however, addresses an important religious concept. God directed Joshua to apportion the land according to those Jews whom God had saved from Egypt. It follows that when a person moves boundary markers in the land of Israel he not only steals but also denies the role of Divine providence in the original setting of boundaries. Thus, this act is doubly forbidden.

By the dual prohibition the Torah highlights both aspects of a forbidden land grab, the civil and the religious. In so doing, the Torah also creates an additional deterrent. Even if the transgressor is a hardened robber who disdains the rights of private property, he may nonetheless refrain from committing an act that denies God's providence in the division of the land.

iv. *A Wise Statute of Limitations*

CONTRARY TO WHAT WE MIGHT EXPECT, THE ATTEMPT TO do harm may elicit a more severe judicial response than the harm or transgression itself. This phenomenon occurs with regard to the prohibition against perjury (19:18-19). "And the judges shall investigate thoroughly, and behold, the witnesses testified falsely, they spoke falsely against their brother. Then you shall do to them as they conspired to do to their brother, and you shall eradicate the evil from your midst."

How do the judges in this case determine that the witnesses perjured themselves? The Talmud (*Makkos* 2a) explains that when two witnesses place the first witnesses in a different location at the very time they claim to have witnessed the crime, the second witnesses are believed. For instance, the second witnesses say, "How could these men have seen the defendant commit murder in New York on Monday afternoon when they were with us in Los Angeles on Monday afternoon?" In this case, the Torah demands that we accept the second witnesses, thereby discrediting the first witnesses and exonerating the defendant. The perjurers then suffer the selfsame punishment the defendant would have suffered had their testimony stood. These perjurers are called *eidim zomemin*, conspiring witnesses.

Strangely, however, this entire process can only take place from the time the court hands down its sentence (*g'mar din*) until it is carried out. The Talmud (*Makkos* 5a) states that if the second witnesses appear after the court has administered its sentence, the first witnesses are not liable to punishment (*kaasher zamam velo kaasher asah*). For instance, if the court has executed the defendant for his crimes, the perjurers receive no punishment.

It is hard to fathom the justice in this detail of the law. Why should God grant immunity from punishment to perjurers if their schemes succeed? Wouldn't that be all the more reason to punish them? The Maharsha suggests that causing the courts to carry out an unjust sentence is too heinous a crime for mere punishment in the courts; only God can deal with criminals of this sort. Perhaps we can offer another suggestion.

The overriding goal of the Torah's legal system is to achieve the closest possible approximation to absolute and comprehensive justice. In the case of false witnesses, perfect justice would demand that they be given a variable punishment, depending on the harm they sought to cause with their testimony. There is, however, a practical difficulty with such a formulation of the law. Since the second, unrebutted witnesses are believed over the first, there would a dangerous opportunity for high mischief. For instance, a disgruntled relative of the executed defendant, whose anger may fester and mushroom over time, may then decide to take the law into his own hands and exact revenge. All he needs to do is find two scoundrels who happen to have been out of sight on the day in question and would, for a few pieces of gold, testify that the first witnesses were with them in a remote place at the time of the crime. Without a statute of limitations, witnesses would forever be vulnerable to this sort of revenge, which is nearly impossible to disprove. A law so structured would discourage truthful witnesses from testifying and forever endanger courageous ones who do. Therefore, the Torah establishes the execution itself as the cutoff for their vulnerability.

Accordingly, the duration of the witnesses' vulnerability is relatively short, from the time the sentence is handed down until it is carried out. If they did indeed perjure themselves, there is enough time for truthful witnesses to come forward and contest their testimony. As for vengeful friends or relatives of the defendant, they are unlikely to be moved to action before the accused is actually convicted, and once he is executed they can no longer do anything. This leaves them with very little time to suborn perjury. Furthermore, from a psychological perspective, the motivation for revenge will not arise until the sentence has actually been carried out, and by then, it is too late to do anything. These laws, therefore, protect the witnesses from attack and allow the legal system to function with maximum integrity.

v. *In the Heat of Battle*

FRUIT TREES, AND BY EXTENSION ALL USEFUL OBJECTS, enjoy the protection of the Torah (20:19-20). "When you besiege a city for many days to wage war against it, to seize it, do not destroy its trees by taking an axe to them, for you eat from it, and you shall not cut it down; is the tree of the field a man that it should enter the siege before you? You may only destroy a tree you know is not a fruit tree, cut it down, and build a bulwark against the city that makes war on you until it is overcome."

Although the context of these verses is war, the Talmud (*Bava Kamma* 91b) derives a prohibition against the wanton destruction of fruit-bearing trees at all times, as well as any item of potential benefit.

Even the briefest glance at these verses raises a host of questions.

Why does the Torah present the prohibition with such elaboration? Why not simply state, "Do not destroy fruit-bearing trees when you besiege a city"?

Why does the Torah employ descriptive phrases such as "for many days" when the prohibition does not depend on the length of the siege? Furthermore, aren't all sieges intended "to seize" the city? Why the redundancy?

Why does the Torah need to present arguments for the protection of the trees by differentiating between trees and people?

Why does the Torah demand we "know" a tree is not fruit-bearing before we may take an axe to it? Isn't that self-understood? After all, does the Torah demand that we "know" an animal is kosher before we eat it?

Why does the Torah instruct that trees that bear no fruit may be cut down for a siege "until [the city] is overcome"? Does this permission depend on the success of the siege?

The Talmud and Midrashim address many of these questions. For example, the *Sifrei* interprets the phrase "many days" as an indication that a siege must begin at least three days before the Sabbath, a law unrelated to the main issue of wanton destruction. Why, however, are these verses so replete with seemingly extraneous information?

Let us take a closer look at the requirement to "know" that a tree is not fruit-bearing before chopping it down. The Talmud (*Bava Kamma* 91b) raises this question and determines that in actuality fruit trees may also be cut down for a siege when there are no other trees to be found. The Malbim, through a precise analysis of the verse, demonstrates that there is a hierarchy even among fruit trees. A person is obliged to "know" through investigation that the fruit tree he is cutting down can no longer bear fruit. He may not cut down an active fruit-bearing tree as long as there are defunct fruit trees to be found. This law is not that dissimilar to other triage decisions a general must make in times of war.

The heat of battle brings out the worst in people. The smell of conquest inflames the warrior's sense of power and importance, and the battle itself unleashes his innate aggressive tendencies. Human emotions once released tend to be fluid, shifting easily from object to object; a parent who had a frustrating day at work may overreact to a child's small misdeed. The Torah, therefore, chooses the highly charged battleground as the venue in which to instruct us on keeping our emotions in check. Even when circumstances permit us to destroy a fruit-bearing tree, we must restrain our aggressive impulses and be discerning in our choices.

Now we may perhaps gain a clearer understanding of the larger framework of the prohibition against wanton destruction. The *Ohr HaChaim*, basing his opinion on the *Zohar*, understands the entire passage as a parable for the relationship between body and soul. Moses stated this law as he neared the end of his life, and he used it to convey important lessons about each individual's battleground — the conduct of his daily life. In this context, the seemingly extraneous words and phrases may be understood as playing a more important role in the metaphor than in the law itself.

The contrast of man and tree highlights the thinly veiled parable Moses was conveying. Although Moses could have made the same points directly, he chose the parable form because of its effectiveness, as would King Solomon centuries later. People find it difficult to face up to their own vices and shortcomings, but they are more receptive to the unthreatening form of a parable. Thus, while instructing the nation not to destroy fruit trees, Moses simultaneously taught the Jewish people for all generations, in the final days of his life, how not to waste their own fruit-bearing lives.

vi. Who Is to Blame?

THE MURDER VICTIM LIES ON THE ROAD. THE MURDERER IS at large and unidentified. Who is to blame? The Torah assigns some blame to the elders of the nearest city. They are required to slaughter a young calf (*eglah arufah*), wash their hands in its blood and declare (21:7), "Our hands have not shed this blood nor have our eyes seen."

The Talmud (*Sotah* 45b) elaborates that these remarks mean that their city did not willfully neglect the needs of this traveler, thereby indirectly contributing to the tragedy. For instance, if the victim had been killed while trying to commit a robbery, the nearby town's supplying him with provisions might have made the attempted crime unnecessary, thereby saving his life. The implication is that a certain amount of responsibility rests on the city elders and by extension on the city itself.

The Torah also assigns a role to the Kohanim in the *eglah aru-*

fah procedure (21:5). "And the Kohanim, the sons of Levi, shall approach, for God your Lord has chosen them to serve Him and bless in the Name of God, and every grievance and plague (*nega*) shall be decided according to their declaration." At this point in the Torah, as we near end of the fifth and final Book, we are already abundantly familiar with the duties of the Kohanim. Nonetheless, the Torah reminds us of three of them — blessing the people in the name of God, adjudicating civil cases and examining lesions on one's body, clothing or house. Why does the Torah recall these functions in the context of this seemingly unrelated law?

If we look closely at these duties we may discern that all three promote social harmony. The ultimate priestly blessing (*Numbers* 6:26) concludes, "May God turn His countenance to you and grant you peace." A *nega* lesion is a consequence of slanderous speech as well as other aggressive acts against others, and its correction brings repentance and reconciliation. Finally, the resolution of civil disputes obviously promotes social harmony. By these three priestly functions, therefore, the Kohanim follow in the footsteps of their ancestor Aaron, who excelled as a peacemaker (*Avos* 1:12).

In the procedure of the *eglah arufah*, there seems to be a certain assignment of responsibility to the Kohanim as well. After the elders wash their hands and make their confession, the Torah calls upon the Kohanim to petition God and say (21:8), "Forgive Your nation Israel that You, God, have redeemed, and do not allow innocent blood in the midst of Your people Israel; and the blood shall be atoned (*nikaper*) for them."

According to the rules of Hebrew grammar, the word for atone should have been *niskaper*, the reflexive form, rather than *nikaper*. In fact, both *Onkelos* and *Targum Yonasan ben Uziel,* in their Aramaic translations, as well as *Ibn Ezra,* translate the word as a reflexive verb. And yet, the verse as it is written seems to be saying, "and we will atone for them with the blood." The subtle implication is that the Kohanim bear a certain responsibility for their failure to promote social harmony adequately, and therefore it is incumbent on them to effect the atonement.

We can also detect a note of criticism in the identification of the Kohanim as "the sons of Levi" in the aftermath of an unsolved murder. In actuality, not all the descendants of Levi are Kohanim, only those descended from Levi's grandson Aaron. Yet here the Torah uncharacteristically refers to them as "the sons of Levi." Perhaps this is an allusion to Levi's role in the slaughter of the entire city of Shechem.

In essence, this short passage underscores the Torah's oft-repeated message that the community and its leaders bear responsibility for the individuals in their midst.

פרשת כי תצא
Parashas Ki Seitzei

i. Of Hair and Nails

ALTHOUGH GENTILE WOMEN ARE FORBIDDEN, THE TORAH makes an exception in times of war (21:10-13). "When you go to war against your enemies . . . and see a beautiful woman (*yefas to'ar*) among the captives, and you desire her, you may take her to wife. Bring her into your home, and she shall cut off her hair and do to her nails . . . and she shall bewail her father and mother for a month, then you may come to her."

The Torah brings the warrior's inflamed, impulse-driven desire under control by establishing a one-month cooling off period during which the captive woman sits in dishevelment and bewails her parents. During this time, "she shall cut off her hair and do to her nails." While the requirement to cut off her hair is unambiguous and clear, what exactly is she supposed to do to her nails?

The Talmud (*Yevamos* 48a) records a dispute on this question. Rabbi Eliezer contends that she must cut her nails. By juxtaposing the nails to the hair, which must be cut off, the Torah undoubtedly wanted that the nails should be cut as well. Rabbi Akiva also notes the juxtaposition of the nails to the hair, but he deduces that she should let her nails grow. Just as cutting off her hair makes the captive woman less attractive, so does letting her nails grow exceedingly long.

Perhaps the underlying argument behind this dispute concerns their understanding of the essential purpose of these laws. According to Rabbi Akiva, these laws serve to remove the Jewish conqueror's desires for his captive. The point of comparison between hair and nails is that they both affect the woman's attractiveness. It is, therefore, logical to deduce that just as cutting off the hair makes her unattractive, doing her nails means letting them grow to make her unattractive.

According to Rabbi Eliezer, however, the purpose of these laws is to condition the pagan captive woman to become a suitable wife for a Jewish man by transforming her emotional framework. She must go through a modified mourning, a liberating catharsis of bewailing her parents, and she must cut off her hair as a symbolic removal of the dead appendages of her previous life, the "dead" religion, the "dead" culture. Consequently, the Torah requires her to cut off her nails as well, since they too are a dead appendage of the body.

ii. *The Seeds of Rebellion*

MODERN PEOPLE WOULD PROBABLY BE SHOCKED BY THE fate of the rebellious son, the *ben sorer umoreh* (21:18-21). "If a man will have a wayward and rebellious son who does not listen to the voice of his father and the voice of his mother . . . [The parents] shall say to the elders of the city, 'This son of ours is wayward and rebellious . . . All the men of his city shall pelt him with stones, and he shall die.'"

They needn't worry. The conditions that had to be met before the death penalty could be administered were so stringent as to make it virtually impossible for it ever to occur. And our Sages indeed assure us that it never did. The Torah's purpose in introducing this law is didactic rather than practical.

The *Midrash Tanchuma* observes that this commandment is the third in the *parashah*. The first is the commandment of *yefas to'ar*, which provides the laws for marrying a heathen woman captured in wartime. The second details the laws of inheritance that apply when a husband has children with two wives, one beloved and one hated. From this sequence, the Midrash infers that a man who marries a heathen captive will come to hate her, and that the union will eventually produce a *ben sorer umoreh*, a rebellious son.

What is the psychology that drives this chain of events?

Perhaps we can find the answer in the story of Amnon and Tamar. Amnon, David's son, harbors a passion for his stepsister Tamar. Unable to restrain himself any longer, he violates her. Afterward, Amnon sends her away; her pleas for him not to do so fall on deaf ears (*II Samuel* 13:15): "Amnon despised her with a great hatred; his hatred was even greater than the love he had felt for her." Amnon hated her because her very presence reminded him of his surrender to his animalistic instincts. Rather than hate himself, he chose to hate the person who reminded him of his vicious act.

In a similar fashion, the Jewish conqueror who succumbs to his lust and marries an unworthy heathen wife may regret his own weaknesses. The Torah predicts that instead of directing his recriminations at himself he will come to hate the wife taken in the moment of his weakness.

Finally, the Midrash suggests, this union may produce a rebellious son. This is not because the heathen wife will fill her son's head with wrong ideas. Wrong ideas do not necessarily lead to rebelliousness; plenty of parents teach their children foolishness and nonsense, and yet the children show no inclination to rebel. The principal causes of rebellion lie elsewhere.

Rebellious children are unhappy children, and the primary source of unhappiness for children is disharmony in the home. Children desperately need the safety and nurturance of a happy home. When they sense tension between parents, their upbringing and happiness are greatly compromised. When a wife is hated and there is acrimony in the home, rebellious children will follow.

iii. Hang the Corpse

CAPITAL PUNISHMENT DOES NOT END WITH THE DEATH OF the lawbreaker. In certain instances, it also requires that his corpse be hanged briefly for public display (21:22-23). "If a man commits a sin punishable by death, he shall be executed, then you shall hang him on a gallows . . . for a hanging person is a curse of the Lord. Do not leave his corpse on the gallows overnight."

The Talmud (*Sanhedrin* 45b) records a dispute between Rabbi Eliezer and the Rabbis regarding the requirement of hanging. According to the Rabbis, only blasphemy demands this procedure. The Rabbis base their view on the words "a hanging person is a curse of the Lord," which teaches that only this grievous violation demands hanging. Rabbi Eliezer contends that all lawbreakers executed by stoning are to be hanged afterward.

There are four forms of capital punishment — stoning, internal immolation, beheading and strangulation. Why would the Torah attach the requirement of hanging the corpse specifically to stoning and not to the other forms of capital punishment?

Moreover, why was Rabbi Eliezer dissatisfied with the Rabbis' simpler interpretation of the verse?

We find frequent mention in the Torah of a punishment serving as a deterrent to others in addition to expiation for the lawbreaker. When people see a person executed, it makes a deep impression and chastens them. Seeing the ultimate consequences of transgression is a powerful deterrent. With regard to this aspect of punishment, stoning falls short.

According to the Talmud, the process of stoning called for pushing the convicted person off a high platform. If he survived, stones were piled on his body until they crushed him to death by their weight. Thus, this is the only one of the four forms of capital punishment during which the public does not actually see the criminal die, unless of course he was killed by the initial fall. Perhaps this is why Rabbi Eliezer understood the verse as teaching that the corpse should be hanged, to give the public the opportunity to observe the results of the execution firsthand and learn from it.

iv. The Promise of Longevity

PROMISES OF LONGEVITY ARE RARE IN THE TORAH. IN FACT, they appear only twice with relation to specific commands. One of these occurs with *shiluach haken*, the sending away of the mother bird before taking the young (22:6-7). "If a bird's nest . . . you shall not take the mother with the young; you shall surely send the mother away and take the young for yourself, so that it will be good for you and you will live a long time." The other is the commandment to honor parents.

The Talmud (*Chullin* 141a) relates a story that raises serious questions about the promised rewards of these commandments.

Elisha ben Avuyah once observed a father telling his son to climb a ladder to a bird's nest and send away the mother bird. The boy fell off the ladder and died. Elisha was stunned. The boy had been fulfilling the two commandments for which the Torah promises goodness and long life. How could he possibly fall to his death while doing these things? And thus Elisha became the famous apostate Acher. The Talmud wonders: Why indeed did this happen? "Good" and "long life," the Talmud explains, refer to the next world, the eternal world of righteous souls, which is all good and endlessly long.

Our Sages state that no verse fully leaves its simple meaning. Perhaps then we may also suggest a more literal interpretation.

King David declares (*Psalms* 89:3) that the world is established through kindness (*olam chessed yibaneh*). God, being perfect and without needs, created the world solely to benefit His creations through His goodness. The ultimate good God allows for us is to be elevated and exalted through a direct relationship with Him. One means of accomplishing this is by imitating His ways; thus, we strive to be kind and merciful just as He is kind and merciful, and thereby, we place our metaphysical souls in harmony with the underlying will of God's *chessed*, the cornerstone of Creation.

By commanding us to have compassion for a bird, a creature with which we have no natural identification, the Torah encourages us to extend our compassionate feelings to all creation and, in doing so, arrive at the level of kindness that is the most fundamental trait of our souls.

The chief beneficiary of this act will not be the bird but rather the person who sends it away. A person who pursues kindness is fully in line with this fundamental trait of his own soul. He will not be disturbed by inner demons of conflict that will drain his life force and age him prematurely. He will achieve the maximum length of days his body will allow; barring mishap, he will have a natural length of days. Moreover, the quality of that life will be far superior to the lives of coarse, selfish people who are in conflict with their souls, which are naturally predisposed to kindness. In this sense, his days will be "good" and "long."

There is a debate among the Sages as to whether the juxtaposition of disparate verses or sections of law in the first four Books of the Torah can be used to derive information or legal principles. All agree, however, that the Book of Deuteronomy may be so expounded. Had Elisha ben Avuyah made a connection between adjacent verses he might have avoided apostasy.

What immediately follows the commandment of sending away the mother bird? It is the commandment of *maakeh*, which calls for the placement of a security fence around an accessible roof. This seems to indicate that even someone who had performed the commandment of *shiluach haken* needs to take precautions against mishaps. Apparently, the promise of good and lengthy days is not a guarantee that no mishaps will occur. It is either a promise of reward in the next world, or an explanation of the profound benefits of such a kindly disposition in this world.

As mentioned above, there is one other commandment for whose fulfillment the Torah promises "good" and "long" days — honoring parents. Can we provide a natural explanation here too according to the simple meaning of the verse? How and why might this transpire?

Honoring parents, the fifth of the Ten Commandments, is the last of the first group, which are generally regarded as sins against God. The Maharal, in *Tiferes Yisrael*, explains that each of these five has a counterpart in the last five commandments, which speak of sins against man.

Violation of the first command by failure to acknowledge God's existence is the equivalent of murder, the sixth. Denying the oneness of God through idols corresponds to the destruction of the oneness of the husband-wife unit through adultery. Misusing God's Name by a false oath is equated with misusing a person in the most basic way — by kidnaping him, the eighth commandment. We give testimony to God's general providence by the observance of the Sabbath, as prescribed by the fourth commandment, so too are we enjoined from giving false testimony against our fellow man, the ninth commandment.

Finally, the commandment to honor parents expresses reverence for and appreciation of God's providence that leads to each individual's own existence. This matches the tenth commandment — not to covet. It would seem that the core failure of covetousness stems from an overestimation of one's importance and a failure to appreciate the blessing of life and everything else God has bestowed. Proper observance leads to gratitude and the conviction that God provides what is appropriate and necessary for satisfaction and happiness in life without having recourse to something belonging to someone else.

Honoring parents shows appreciation for the vehicle God chose for drawing our Divine souls into our bodies, the individual providence of our own existence. Appreciation, *hakaras hatov*, is like the kindness essential for a person's *sh'leimus* (wholeness or perfection). It allows a person to be satisfied or happy with his lot. Thus, like sending the mother bird away, it is "good for him" and "lengthens his days."

v. *Two Seeds and a Fence*

WHEN TWO LAWS APPEAR NEXT TO EACH OTHER, IT IS SUGgestive. When they seem unrelated and are paired together as the only two laws in a section, they cry out for interpretation (22:8-9). "When you build a new house, make a fence for your roof, so that you will not cause bloodshed in your house should an unsteady person fall from it. You shall not sow your vineyard with a mixture lest the growth of the seed you plant and the produce of the vineyard become forbidden." What is the connection between these two laws?

The commandment prohibiting the mixed planting of different seeds (*kilayim*) is difficult to categorize. Does it enhance our relationship with God? With other people? Does it lead to personal perfection? In Leviticus (19:19), when the Torah first mentions the commandment of *kilayim*, *Ibn Ezra* comments that *kilayim* serves as a reminder that the perfect person's greatness lies in that he does not follow his emotional inclinations when they contradict his rational thought; he does not mix the two.

The Torah's use of mixing seeds (according to the oral tradition, this refers specifically to grains) and wine fits well with this approach. Wine, which causes man to lose his inhibitions, represents emotional man. Grain represents rational man; it is the first goal of human industry and reflects man's intelligence; our Sages state (*Berachos* 40a) that a child does not distinguish between mother and father until he eats grains. Thus, the prohibition against mixing grains and wine is an apt metaphor for the need to shield rational thought from potentially distorting emotional inclinations.

The juxtaposition then suggests that just as surely as we should create a protective fence to protect against physical harm (*maakeh*), so too should we create a spiritual protective fence to protect our rational thoughts from the emotional drives that can corrupt them and cause harm.

vi. Free to Gladden

PARADOXICALLY, THE TORAH FIRST PRESENTS THE LAWS OF divorce and only afterwards the laws pertaining to newlywed couples (24:1-6). "If a man marries a woman and lives with her, and if it should happen that she does not find favor in his eyes . . . then he will write her a bill of divorce . . . When a man takes a new wife, he shall not go out to the army, nor shall it obligate him for any matter; he shall be free for his home for one year, and he shall gladden his wife that he has taken. He shall not take a lower or upper millstone as a pledge, for he would be taking a life as a pledge."

It would seem that the Torah employs this sequence to tell us how to avoid divorce; once the Torah explicates the laws of divorce, it gives us the antidote that will protect against this awful scourge. But how specifically does having the groom totally free to gladden his wife during the first year of marriage help in avoiding divorce? And what does any of this have to do with not taking a millstone as a pledge, which appears in the next verse without any separation?

We may begin to answer by asking further: Why does the burden of prevention fall on the husband? According to Jewish thought, the psychological relationship between a husband and wife is asymmetrical. In a certain sense, the woman's *raison d'être*, according to the story of Eve's creation, is to be a help to her husband (*eizer kenegdo*); her very name derives from his (*ishah* from *ish*). It follows that an important aspect of a woman's spiritual or psychological contentment stems from the feeling that she helps her husband and pleases him. If so, wouldn't it make more sense for the Torah to require the marriage to be set on course by her pleasing him?

In telling us that a groom must be "free" to gladden his wife, the Torah rather strangely uses the word *naki*, whose literal translation is "clean." Apparently, the Torah is telling us that a woman's devotion to her husband is in part responsive; it occurs only when he is "clean" to her. She responds to his personal integrity by respecting him and becoming increasingly devoted to him. Furthermore, his attention to her from the inception of the marriage provides her an important sense of security, which causes her to reciprocate with her own devotion.

Adam acceded to Eve's suggestion that he eat the forbidden

fruit. According to the Midrashim, this sin stemmed in part from inadequate control of their baser drives. With regard to Adam, who had listened to his wife, God addressed this issue by decreeing that henceforth man would "eat bread" by the sweat of his brow. As a result of the curse, some of Adam's energy, would now be scattered. Man's mental energy would no longer find full satisfaction unless it was partially sublimated in his conquest of his external world. In fact, even his marital relationship would depend on his labors. There is an allusion to this in the language of the verse, which states that he will eat "bread" by the sweat of his brow, "bread" being a euphemism for wife (*Genesis* 39:6; *Rashi*). Following Adam's sin, man's satisfaction in his relationship with his wife is also dependent on his feeling a sense of accomplishment or conquest in his external world.

The continuation of the verses immediately leads us into a seemingly unrelated law prohibiting the appropriation of millstones as a pledge for a loan. *Targum Yonasan,* however, states specifically that there is a connection. Perhaps it is because the millstones represent the tools of a man's livelihood, the items he needs to succeed in his conquests outside the home and to ensure that his wife feels secure within.

vii. *More on Marriage and Millstones*

ONCE AGAIN, WE FIND TWO SEEMINGLY UNRELATED COMmandments encapsulated together in one section, marked by a *stumah* gap before and after (24:5-6). "When a man takes a new wife, he shall not go out to the army, nor shall it obligate him for any matter; he shall be free for his home for one year, and he shall gladden his wife that he has taken. He shall not take a lower or upper millstone as a pledge, for he would be taking a life as a pledge." What is the connection between taking a grindstone as a pledge in a loan and a groom's obligation to cement the bonds of marriage?

Furthermore, why does the Torah single out a millstone as the item that must not be taken as a pledge for a loan? Why would a lender interested in ensuring the repayment of his loan deprive the borrower of the very article that will provide him with a livelihood?

Let us take a look at *Targum Yonasan's* enigmatic Midrashic translation of this verse. "Do not take a man's upper or lower millstone as a pledge, for his livelihood depends on it, and do not separate a bride from a groom with magic, for by so doing, the souls that would be born [by the union] are destroyed." *Targum Yonasan* clearly connects this verse to the previous one, but how taking a millstone relates to separating newlyweds by magic remains unexplained.

We find that a person may derive a vicarious pleasure in that area in which he controls another. The Talmud (*Shabbos* 55b) explains that when scripture states that the sons of Eli the Kohen Gadol had relations with women who came to offer sacrifices at shiloh, no adultry ever occurred. Eli's sons did, however, intentionally delay the return of these women to their husbands by withholding the bringing of their sacrifices overnight. The verse's reference indicates that this delay tantamount to illicit relations. What does this mean? How can an overnight delay in the sacrifices be compared to carnal relations?

The answer lies in that faculty of the human personality that derives a libidinous pleasure from the control over another person's ability to have relations. This capacity stems from man's basest instinct and his desire for mastery and conquest, which are fluidly linked in the human psyche.[1] Therefore, there must

1. This linkage already appears in God's first command to Adam to populate the earth and subdue it. The Vilna Gaon, in his commentary on Proverbs, identifies the two most basic biological drives in man as desire (*taavah*) and aggression (*kinah*), the inclinations propelling reproduction and conquest.

have been some inappropriate element on the part of Eli's sons if they delayed the return of the women to their husbands. Scripture makes this point with its stark accusation of illicit relations against these otherwise righteous men.

In this light, we can perhaps discern the connection between taking control of the tools of someone's livelihood and interference in the marital relationship. Someone who would take a millstone as a pledge is not motivated by the security of his loan, since he is actually hindering the borrower's ability to repay it. Rather, he is driven by a primitive desire for pleasure by exercising control over another man. A person's corrupt desire to exercise power and control over another finds its maximum expression in separating newlyweds when their attraction is greatest, thereby gaining sublimated illicit pleasure for himself.

viii. *Don't Muzzle the Animals*

IN THE TORAH, CRIME DEMANDS CONSEQUENCES, FREquently punishment. Commonly, this takes the form of lashes (25:3). "Forty shall he strike him, he shall not add, lest he strike him an additional blow beyond these, and your brother will be degraded in your eyes."

The Torah does not explicitly specify, however, which violations are punishable by lashes. The *Sifrei* (26) derives the parameters from the juxtaposition of the law prescribing lashes and the prohibition against muzzling an animal while it threshes grain. All those transgressions similar to this transgression (*lav d'chasimah*) are punishable by lashes.

There are, of course, scores of transgressions the Torah could have chosen to serve as a model. Why does the Torah pick this one? The question is strengthened by the absence of a spacing divider (*stumah*) between these two seemingly unrelated laws.

When a man muzzles his animal during threshing to prevent it from eating, he shows himself to be at the very least insensitive to the animal's plight; he feels so superior to it that he has no remorse in torturing this subhuman creature. In administering lashes, the Torah is also concerned about callous superiority, as the verse concludes, "He shall not add, lest he strike him an additional blow beyond these, and your brother will be degraded in your eyes." We are enjoined against feeling superior to the condemned violator. He remains our brother whose shame must be mitigated. The juxtaposition underscores this awareness.

ix. The Roots of Embarrassment

ON RARE OCCASIONS, THE TORAH EXPRESSES ITSELF IN FIGurative terms. The law of damages provides a prime example (25:11-12). "If men fight with one another, a man and his brother, and the wife of one of them approaches to rescue her husband from his assailant, and she stretches out her hand and grasps his privates, you shall cut off her hand; your eyes shall not show pity."

According to our oral tradition, we do not chop off the woman's hand for causing embarrassment to another person. The Talmud (*Bava Kamma* 27a) makes it abundantly clear that she compensates with money. If so, why does the Torah express this monetary obligation in such graphic terms? Finally, how does this law fit into the sequence of laws presented here?

Let us consider the two laws that precede this law. First is the law of the administration of lashes as punishment for certain transgressions. This is followed by the law of *chalitzah*, the ritual whereby a widow removes her brother-in-law's shoe and spits on the ground in front of him, in order to avoid Levirate marriage. Both of these laws have an important aspect of embarrassment. The law of lashes concludes with the commandment not to administer excessive punishment lest the recipient be embarrassed (25:3). The *chalitzah* procedure ends with the declaration that the household of the man who fails to marry his brother's widow should be known in shame as *beis chalutz hanaal*, "the house of the removed shoe."

We begin to discern a logical flow to these seemingly unrelated laws. The first prescribes lashes, which may cause embarrassment. The second is specifically designed to embarrass. Nonetheless, embarrassment is a serious matter and must not be taken lightly. Therefore, the Torah immediately and graphically declares that the damages of embarrassment are real and require reparation.

By expressing the punishment in such harsh terms, that the offender's hand is cut off, the Torah emphasizes that the harm caused through embarrassment is no less real than physical damage. In fact, the harm is so severe that its victim's sense of justice cries out for the offending hand to be severed. The Torah, however, does not sanction dismemberment and imposes monetary penalties instead.

x. *Amalek and Honest Weights*

FORTY YEARS AFTER THE EVENT TOOK PLACE, GOD instructed the Jewish people to destroy Amalek (25:17-19). "Remember what Amalek did to you along the way when you were leaving Egypt, that he happened upon you along the way and he struck those of you who lagged behind, when you were faint and exhausted, and he did not fear the Lord. And it shall be that when God your Lord gives you rest from all your surrounding enemies in the land God your Lord gives you as an inheritance to possess it, you shall wipe out the memory of Amalek from under the heavens — do not forget!"

Amalek's attack is described in Exodus (17:14). At the time, God did not instruct the Jewish people to carry out the destruction of Amalek. Instead, He assured them that He would. What changed in the course of the forty years so that He now commands the nation to be His warring emissaries?

Most likely, the change was in the level of the Jewish people themselves. Preceding the attack of the Amalekites, the people had lacked water, and they had tested God by wondering, "Is God among us or not?" Forty years later, they had evolved. The commandment to keep honest weights and measures immediately precedes the commandment to destroy Amalek. The juxtaposition suggests that the people acknowledged God's presence in their midst by observing these commandments, since only God knows if a person has shaved a stone. By dealing faithfully with each other and God, as reflected in honest weights and measures, they acknowledged His presence in their midst. This is the condition upon which God could give them the obligation and opportunity to eradicate the nation that denies the reality of God's existence and the ethical conduct He demands.

In this light, we can understand why the commandment to destroy Amalek comes into effect only after God alleviates the pressure "from all your surrounding enemies." Wouldn't it have been useful and desirous to eradicate this implacable enemy of the Jewish people and God as soon as possible?

The absence of enemies clearly establishes that the war against Amalek is not fought for safety. We fight with no other purpose than to rid the world of Amalek, the people antithetically opposed to Israel's Divine mission, in their denial of God, His will and His providence. Therefore, this war must be fought at a time when the Jewish people are at peace. If they then initiate the battle, it is clear that they are doing so only because Amalek embodies traits and values that cannot be allowed to survive, even as a memory.

פרשת כי תבא
Parashas Ki Savo

i. Thanks for the Fruit

EVERY YEAR, WHEN THE FIRST FRUITS APPEARED, THE landowner would bring them to the Temple in Jerusalem and make a special declaration (26:1-10). "And it will be when you enter the land that God your Lord gives you as an inheritance . . . then you shall take of the first of every fruit of the earth that you bring forth from your land that God your Lord gives you . . . Then you shall call out and say before God your Lord, 'An Aramean tried to destroy my forefather [Jacob]. He descended to Egypt and sojourned there, few in number, and there he became a nation, great, strong and numerous... and now behold I have brought the first fruits of the ground You have given me, O God.'" This declaration is known as *Vidui Bikkurim*, the Confession Over the First Fruit.

The question naturally arises: What is so monumental about this offering that it should call for such an elaborate recital?

The Talmud (*Rosh Hashanah* 43b) states that upon seeing the first blossoms of a fruit tree in the spring we must bless God "Who did not leave anything lacking from His universe, and created in it good creations and good trees with which to cause pleasure to mankind." Once again, we encounter an unusually elaborate blessing over fruit. More curiously, the blessing acknowledges God as the source of the pleasures we will have from the fruit tree only much later. Why did our Sages institute the blessing well in advance of the benefit we will derive from it? In fact, our Sages generally require that there be no interruptions between a blessing over a pleasure and the experience of the pleasure itself.

Of all naturally existing foodstuffs, fruit is unique in that it provides pure palliative pleasure. Even when our hunger is sated, we still find room for a fruit because of its delicious taste. In this sense, fruits represent a pleasure that is not necessary for our basic sustenance, a bonus from God that attests to His benevolence. Upon seeing the first bud of a fruit tree, we are reminded of His benevolent nature. We recognize that He created a world that provides not only our needs but also contains objects that exist only for our pleasure. And we bless Him for it.

Likewise, this reality underscores the Temple declaration over God's enveloping benevolence — our redemption from Egypt, the gift of His holy Torah, the gift of the land of Israel. Appropriately, we express these thoughts when we bring the first fruit. This is when we should feel the greatest surge of *hakaras hatov*, recognition and appreciation of God's benevolence.

ii. Gaze Down Blessings

AFTER THE THIRD AND SIXTH YEARS OF THE SEVEN-YEAR agricultural cycle, the Jewish landowner made a declaration that he had fulfilled all his obligations for agricultural tithes. He then petitioned God for His blessing (26:12-15).

"When you have finished tithing every tithe of your produce in the third year, the year of the tithes, you shall give to the Levites, to the proselytes, to the orphan and to the widow, and they shall eat in your citadels and be satisfied. Then you shall say before God your Lord, 'I removed the holy things from the house, I have given it to the Levites, to the proselytes, to the orphan and to the widow, according to whatever commandments You have commanded me . . . Gaze down from Your holy abode, from the heavens, and bless Your people Israel and the earth You have given us . . ."

Although the expression "gaze down" seems innocuous, it is really quite ominous. Rashi comments (*Genesis* 18:16), "Every mention of 'gazing' (*hashkafah*) in Scripture connotes something bad, except in the verse 'gaze down from Your holy abode' . . . for so great is the power of giving to the poor that it transforms God's anger into mercy."

Granted that the word gaze in this case has been transformed into an expression of mercy, as Rashi indicates, still, why did the Torah choose to have the landowner ask for God's blessing with that particular word? Why not petition for a "looking" with no negative connotations?

The Midrash comments that the account of creation begins with the exclusive use of *Elo-him,* the Name that refers to God's attribute of *din*, strict justice. Only afterward is the Tetragrammaton, the Name that refers to His attribute of mercy, attached to it. The Midrash explains that God initially intended to create the world according to *din*. When He saw that man could not withstand such a high standard, He added the quality of mercy (*rachamim*).

Ultimately, then, the world was created through a combination of strict justice and mercy. In His infinite wisdom, God determined that man would benefit most from fulfilling His will according to the letter of the law (*din*). In this circumstance, man is most responsible for his actions and thereby gains the most benefit for his soul through free-willed moral choices. However, man is unable to attain this ideal potential; therefore, God introduced the attribute of mercy (*rachamim*) in the equation of man's judgment. The result of this combination of attributes is that God tempers His judgment, delaying or meting out punishment piecemeal in order to allow penitence to modify the judgment. According to our Sages, mankind in the Messianic era will reach a level of existence high enough to live according to the attribute of *din*, which is the ultimate Divine kindness in that it maximizes the benefit man can attain through his free choices.

At the end of the three-year agricultural cycle, the Jewish landowner declares that he has properly used the physical bounties God has bestowed upon him, that he has fulfilled his obligations of kindness and generosity to his fellow man. Within this framework of correctly fulfilling God's purpose in creation, man is entitled to ask for God's further blessing even according to the highest level of existence, which is strict justice, *din*. By saying "gaze down" he invokes the attribute of strict justice and demonstrates that he has transformed his own existence and earned the right to God's kindness.

iii. *Mammoth Mezuzos*

UPON ENTRY INTO THE LAND, GOD REQUIRED THAT THE Jewish people immediately erect megaliths (27:2-3). "And it shall be on the day that you cross the Jordan to the land that God your Lord gives you, then you shall erect for yourselves great stones and coat them with plaster. And you shall inscribe upon them all the words of this Torah when you cross over . . ." What was the purpose of these megaliths?

Man has several layers of protection. The skin covers the entire body. Clothes cover the skin. Houses protect us from the elements. The Torah gave us commandments and signs that relate to each of these concentric layers of protection. The commandment of *milah*, circumcision, places the sign of the covenant in the skin itself. The *tefillin* contain fundamental concepts of God, and we lay them directly on the skin. We place *tzitzis*, fringes, on our garments as a sign of our providential redemption. The *mezuzah* also contains fundamental concepts of God, and we affix it as a sign on the doorpost of the house. In this way, we underscore that our true security is not in any of these physical environmental layers but in our relationship with God.

As the Jewish people stood ready to enter the land of Israel, the new home of the nation, they were about to add yet another layer of protection — the land. Here, too, God commanded them to erect megaliths and inscribe the Torah upon them. The giant stones would serve as mammoth *mezuzos* stating the true purpose for which God gave the Jewish people the land.

In this light, perhaps we can find additional insight into a famous ruling of the Talmud (*Sanhedrin* 74a) regarding tying one's shoes. Generally, we give preference to the right side, because it reminds us of God's right hand, which administers mercy. In tying our shoes, our custom, which has become law, is to tie the left shoe first, because this reminds us of the *tefillin* we wear on the left arm. The Sages single out this seemingly picayune protocol of haberdashery as an example of a law that must be observed meticulously even during a widespread campaign to subvert Judaism (*shmad*). If a person is ordered to tie his right shoe first on pain of death, he must give up his life before violating even this minor law.

Can we add any depth as to why this particular law is singled out as the example of one that must be kept at all costs, beyond its obvious triviality?

Perhaps we can suggest that, while the obligation to die for the Torah in such dire times certainly applies to any and all laws, there is an additional significance to this law that brings it to the fore. Tying one's shoes is generally the last act of dressing, and as such, it conceptually encapsulates all our clothing. Therefore, we are required to draw a parallel between the clothing and the *tefill-*

in that are also placed on our bodies and also tied on the left, thereby recalling the ultimate concepts of our protection contained in these boxes. In so doing, we remind ourselves that our relationship with God provides our only true protection.

We may offer yet another significance to this law. Tying our shoes on the left is an exception to the general rule that gives precedence to the right. It is a consoling reminder that times of national devastation and punishment, as represented by the left, are the exception and that God's mercy, as represented by the right, is the general rule that will prevail.

פרשת נצבים
Parashas Nitzavim

i. No More Shortcuts

ON THE DAY OF HIS DEATH, MOSES DELIVERS HIS FINAL ORATORY to the Jewish people (29:9-10). "You are standing today, all of you, before God your Lord, the heads of your tribes, your elders and your officers, all the men of Israel, your small children, your women, and your proselytes who are in the midst of your camp, from your woodcutters to your water carriers."

Who were these "woodcutters and water carriers"? *Midrash Tanchuma* identifies them as Canaanites who having heard of Israel's battlefield success had recently come forward to convert. The verse also mentions other "proselytes," yet these Canaanite woodcutters and water carriers are grouped separately, indicating that Moses had relegated them to a lower, servile status. They were accepted as converts but not fully integrated with the nation as were the other earlier converts; their status was similar to the *ger toshav*, the resident alien who observes the seven Noahide laws.

The Midrash (*Midrash Rabbah* 42:6) points out that Moses had erred in accepting full conversion of the *eiruv rav*, the mixed multitude of Egyptians who joined the Jewish people at the time of the Exodus. God had advised him to defer their conversion, but Moses, in his love for humanity, had mistakenly tried to expedite the process of history whose goal is that all people gain knowledge of God.

Forty years later, Moses had learned his lesson. The Jewish people had suffered interminably from the depredations of the *eiruv rav*. Now, when these Canaanites sought conversion, Moses was not so forthcoming. He designated them as woodcutters and water carriers, not allowing them full membership in the Jewish people. There would be no more shortcuts to the final redemption of all mankind. It would have to be accomplished in steps.

ii. Subtle Suggestions

MOSES EXPECTS THE ENLIGHTENED JEWISH PEOPLE TO THINK back with derision to the icons of the pagans they encountered both in Egypt and in the desert (29:16-17). "And you have seen their abominations and detestable idols of wood and stone, of silver and gold that were with them. Perhaps there is among you . . . whose heart turns away today from God our Lord to go to worship the gods of the nations . . ."

Why does Moses find it necessary to specify the various material from which the idols were constructed? Furthermore, why separate the list of materials into two groupings, "wood and stone" and "silver and gold"?

People generally judge by appearances. It takes a special inner strength to penetrate the facade and investigate the underlying essence of people or things. It was quite obvious that the enlightened people of the desert would instantly dismiss as nonsense any cult they encountered that conducted ridiculous rites in decrepit hovels. But what if these selfsame practices were conducted in magnificent gilded cathedrals attended by well-dressed and dignified personages? Would the people as easily recognize and reject the falsity of the core beliefs? It would likely be more difficult.

Perhaps this was the message Moses intended to convey. Just as icons of sticks and stones are easily recognized as ridiculous, so must the more appealingly adorned nonsense of silver and gold be recognized as such.

After speaking disdainfully of the old idols, Moses issues a warning to those who may turn from God "to go to worship the gods of the nations." Why does he insert the seemingly superfluous "to go"? Why isn't it enough to warn against worshiping these foreign gods?

People of conscience do not generally tolerate a complete break from their principles to lust after their desires. Initially, they slide toward sin and hover around it. Their mental energies and interests anticipate the forbidden pleasure, but conscience or guilt holds them back. So they compromise. For instance, they may allow their gaze to linger inappropriately, but they stop at that. Still, in so doing they have already crossed a proscribed threshold. They have already started "to go" toward sin. This threshold will now be more easily crossed next time, and the battle of conscience will take place deeper into the realm of sin.

This is a commonplace mechanism of sin. People "go" and "worship" their idols. This mechanism is both a curse and blessing. It weakens the defenses, but it staves off the act. It allows people the opportunity to examine their inclinations and leanings. It allows them to head sin off at the pass.

iii. *The Divine Prod*

Only ten of the hundreds of thousands of letters of the Torah are written in an unusually large fashion. In some of these instances, we have unfortunately lost the tradition as to what their unusual size signifies, and we are left to muse about God's message on our own.

In this parashah, we have such an unexplained letter. Moses predicts that God will exile the Jewish people and that the devastation of the land of Israel will attest to the Divine hand in these happenings. Observers will remark (29:27), "And God removed them from their soil, with anger, with wrath, and with great fury, and He cast them away (*vayashlichem*, וַיַּשְׁלִכֵם) to another land as on this very day."

What is the significance of this large letter *lamed* (ל)? Literally, the *lamed* means both "to teach" and "a prod." Kabbalistic literature offers additional insight into the symbol of the letter *lamed* for teaching. The *lamed* is formed with a high ascender that extends well above the roofline of the Hebrew alphabet. This connotes Divine instruction.

In this light, we may interpret the large letter *lamed* in the verse that describes the protracted calamity befalling the Jewish people. By calling attention to itself, the large *lamed* declares that even in our misfortune there remains a Divine connection. God's apparent wrath is a Divine instruction, a prod for our benefit to induce us to turn away from iniquity and return to Him. This theme recurs frequently in the Bible and in rabbinic writings. At the burning bush, God told Moses that His name is *Ek-eh Asher Ek-eh* (I Will Be What I Will Be). As quoted in Rashi, the Midrash (*Shemos Rabbah* 3:6) explains this as "just as I am with the Jewish people in their current suffering in Egypt, so too will I be with them in all future sufferings." God will temper our torment to that which is beneficial and bearable. He will prod and teach us at the same time.

We may further suggest than the large *lamed* also encourages us to divide the word *vayashlichem* (וַיַּשְׁלִכֵם) into two parts. We may read it homiletically as *veyesh* (וְיֵשׁ), "and there is," and *lachem* (לָכֶם), "to you." The word *yesh* (יֵשׁ) also means existence. Read this way, the verse assures us that God's punishment is actually a form of His hidden mercy, because it preserves our eternal existence before our corruption leads to spiritual self-annihilation.

We find another enigma in the verse's concluding words, "He cast [the Jewish people] to another land as on this very day (*kayom hazeh*)." To which "very day" is Moses referring here?

These words were uttered on the seventh of Adar, the last day of Moses' life. On the morrow, Joshua would assume leadership of the nation and shortly thereafter bring them into the land. On that very day, as Moses bid the nation farewell and the people prepared to enter the land, God promises that He will just as immediately cast them out — if that is what it takes to preserve the sanctity of the nation.

iv. *The Push and Pull of Return*

AFTER THE EXILE, GOD PROMISES TO BRING THE PEOPLE back to the land (30:3-5). "Then God your Lord will bring back your captives and have mercy upon you, and He will gather you from all the peoples among whom God your Lord has scattered you. And if your dispersed will be at the end of heaven, God your Lord will gather you in from there and He will take you from there. Then God your Lord will bring you to the land your forefathers possessed and you shall possess it."

Shortly before the turn of the 20th century, not even one-ten-thousandth of world Jewry lived in the land of Israel. About a hundred years later, it is estimated that about 35 percent of all Jews live in Israel. Moreover, demographers and sociologists further estimate that by early in the 21st century it will surpass 50 percent, as relatively higher birthrates in Israel, further immigration to Israel, and higher intermarriage in the Diaspora will shift the balance to make Israel the physical center of Jewish life. Is this a precursor to the final redemption? Rabbis offer differing views on this sensitive issue. All agree, however, that the Divine hand guided the dramatic transformation of the 20th century. Surely, if this is not the beginning of the final ingathering, it foreshadows it.

Ironically, the common denominator of most of the migrations has been that, although the vast majority of immigrants have been happy to return to their ancestral homeland, the push to leave their former place of residence motivated them more than the pull of Israel. This is true for the Jews driven from Europe by the Holocaust, those who fled persecution in the Arab lands after Israel's War of Independence, anti-Semitism in South America, economic hardship and persecution in the Soviet Union, the breakdown of civil order in South Africa and starvation in Ethiopia. If not for the push of circumstances, few of these Jews would have migrated, even if given the opportunity. However all this fits into the Divine master plan; we can see the hand of God guiding the history of our people.

There is another aspect to this influx that has Biblical roots. When the Jewish people left Egypt, many non-Jews hitched their wagons to the express train of the Jewish people as they burst out of Egypt. They are called the *eiruv rav*, mixed multitude. According to our Sages, Moses' acceptance of these fair-weather converts caused numerous problems during the forty years in the desert and beyond. The most recent wave of immigration to Israel is vexed with the same problem of large numbers of non-Jews in their midst, especially among the immigrants from the former Soviet Union. Furthermore, if events drive large numbers of Jewish people to Israel from the Western democracies, where intermarriage rates are approaching 50 percent, they will supplement the already large *eiruv rav* in Israel today and further undermine the Jewish character of Israeli society.

Our daily prayers acknowledge the difficulty of the return of the Jewish people and that it does not occur naturally. The prayer for the ingathering of our exiles is the only one of the nineteen in the *Amidah* which petitions God for a miracle (*nes*) to accomplish our request, stating, "[Perform] a miracle to gather us in from our places of exile (נֵס לְקַבֵּץ גָּלֻיּוֹתֵינוּ)."

פרשת וילך
Parashas Vayeilech

The Torah as Poetry

MOSES INSTRUCTS THE JEWISH PEOPLE TO WRITE AND TEACH a *shirah*, which is a song or a poem (31:19). "So now write for yourselves this song (*shirah*), and teach it to the people of Israel, placing it in their mouths so that this song shall be a witness for Me among the people of Israel."

To what does this refer? According to Rashi, it refers to the poetic message of *Parashas Haazinu,* which comes immediately afterward and appears in the Torah in poetic form, with line breaks following meter. The Talmud (*Sanhedrin* 21b), however, explains that the term *shirah* refers to the entire Torah. In what way is the Torah considered *shirah*, song?

Song refers to a composition expressing facts, ideas or emotions in a style more concentrated, imaginative and powerful than ordinary speech. The singular style in which the Torah is written meets and exceeds all these conditions.

According to our oral tradition, Moses transcribed every letter of the Torah precisely as God willed it (*aspaklaria me'irah*). More than by content alone, the Torah conveys ideas by numerous literary devices, which in total are found in no other known document. Among these are:

- *Cantillation marks* that modulate the tone and cadence of the reading.
- *Gaps in spacing* between segments, such as *stumah* (closed), *pesuchah* (open) and *shirah* (poetry).
- *Juxtaposition* of verses and concepts to convey added meaning.
- *Inconsistencies* and anomalies in grammar and syntax.
- *Text markings*, such as odd-sized, inverted or dotted letters.
- *Oral traditions* in reading words other than as written (*kri-ksiv*).
- *Gematria*, which assigns a numerical value to each letter in the Hebrew alphabet, thereby creating connections among words or phrases.
- *Resonant language*, by which the Torah will employ a word repeatedly, often a significant number of times, in one passage or in related passages to convey an extra level of meaning.

This unparalleled array of literary devices which conveys the Torah's meaning to us allows us to glimpse a fragment of the infinite wisdom of its Author. It is easily understood then how the whole Torah is poetry.

פרשת האזינו
Parashas Haazinu

The Creation Letter

ONCE AGAIN, THE TORAH EMPLOYS THE DEVICE OF AN oversized letter, this time the *hei* (ה) that begins the following verse, to send us a subtle message (32:6). "Is it to God (הַ לַה') that you do this, O vile and unwise people? Is He not your Father, your Master? Has He not created and prepared you?" What is the significance of the enlarged *hei*?

Perhaps we can find a clue in the only other instance of an odd-sized *hei*, which occurs at the opposite end of the Torah (*Genesis* 2:4). "These are the generations of heaven and earth when they were created on the day that God the Lord made earth and heaven." The letter *hei* in the word *behibar'am*, "when they were created," is undersized. Our Sages see this as a cryptic hint that God created the world with the letter *hei*.

There are profound and esoteric concepts underlying this Midrash. According to Kabbalistic thought, the numerical value of *hei*, which is 5, is significant. For example, there are 5 worlds of creation (*asiah*, *beriah*, *yetzirah*, *atzilus, adam hakadmon*) just as there are 5 levels of the soul (*nefesh, ruach, neshamah, chayah, yechidah*). Man, whose creation is an echo of the blueprint of the universe, has 5 digits on each of his limbs, 5 senses, 5 orifices. The Torah is also divided into 5 parts and 5 commandments appeared on each of the Tablets. The Kabbalists also find profound meaning in the very shape of the letter *hei*.

Granted that the unusual size of the *hei* alludes to its dominant role in creation, why then is it undersized? One might have thought that the primacy of the letter, as reflecting creation, would be better suited to be oversized.

Perhaps we can glimpse the answer if we view the two appearances of the odd-sized *hei* together. In both instances, Genesis and Deuteronomy, there is a reference to creation. In Genesis, the verse describes the underlying blueprint for creation, which is hidden from mankind; the *hei* is consequently small. In Deuteronomy, the verse also refers to God as man's Creator and conveys the thought that it is therefore audacious for man to disregard his obligations. By Deuteronomy, God's design in creating man has been clearly revealed through the Torah; the *hei* is consequently large.

פרשת וזאת הברכה

Parashas Vezos HaBerachah

i. Changing the Order

JUST AS THE BOOK OF GENESIS CONCLUDES WITH JACOB blessing his children, so does the Book of Deuteronomy conclude with Moses blessing the Jewish people (33:1). "And this is the blessing that Moses, the man of God, bestowed upon the people of Israel before his death."

There are many similarities in the content of these specific blessings, and also differences. One difference is in the order in which they are given. Jacob blesses his sons according to their birth order, with one exception. Jacob blessed all his sons from Leah before proceeding to the next born from Bilhah, Rachel's handmaiden.

Two hundred and fifty years later, with the roles of the tribes more highly defined, Moses chooses a different order. What principles guided Moses' ordering of the blessings?

At first, Moses blessed Reuven, the eldest son. Shimon, the second born to Jacob, should have followed Reuven. But he didn't. Rashi explains that Moses excluded Shimon from an expressed blessing because of the tribe's involvement in the licentiousness and idolatry at Baal Peor; nonetheless, Shimon was included in Judah's blessing, just as his portion in Israel is completely contained within Judah's borders. Judah, the fourth son, thus moved up and received the second blessing in place of Shimon. He was followed by Levi, the third born.

At this point, Levi had already been designated to serve in the *Mishkan* and later in the Temple, which was located in Benjamin's portion for 830 years. This functional relationship between Levi and Benjamin dictated that Benjamin should be mentioned next. Joseph followed immediately afterward, because the *Mishkan* resided for 369 years in Shiloh, in the portion of Ephraim, one of Joseph's sons. The tribe of Joseph may also have followed Benjamin because they were both descended from Rachel or else because they were the most distinguished of the remaining tribes.

After Joseph, Moses continued blessing the tribes derived from Leah's biological sons according to their birth orders. He then proceeded to bless Gad, the older son of Leah's handmaiden Zilpah. One might have expected Naphtali, Zilpah's second son, to be blessed next to complete the blessing of Leah's children. Moses chose instead to bless Dan, the older son of Bilhah, Rachel's handmaiden. Perhaps this was because of Dan's special status as leader of the three tribes located to the north of the Mishkan in the desert encampment — Dan, Naphtali and Asher. Moses then blessed Naphtali and concluded with Asher, Bilhah's younger son, the last born of the handmaidens' children.

Yet another subtle discrepancy between Jacob's and Moses' blessings may shed further light on the logic of Moses' order. When Jacob blesses each of his eight sons by Rachel and Leah, his two chief wives, the Torah marks off each blessing with a *pesuchah*, the maximum spacing between verses.[1] However, the blessings to the sons of Bilhah and Zilpah, Jacob's concubines, are sandwiched tightly between the blessings to Leah's and Rachel's

1. In contrast to a *stumah*, which demands only the equivalent of four letter-sized blank spaces, a *pesuchah* leaves blank the remainder of the line on which a verse ends.

descendants. A smaller *stumah* gap separates these blessings from each other and from the blessings that precede and follow them. In contrast, Moses blesses the four tribes descended from the concubines last, and with one exception, a smaller *stumah* gap separates the blessings to all the tribes from each other.

Perhaps we may suggest that when Jacob initially blessed his children, the sons of the concubines were of secondary status, so to speak, to the sons of Leah and Rachel. Therefore, Jacob sandwiched their blessings among the blessings to the others and delineated them with smaller *stumah* gaps, reflecting their ancillary status and dependency.

When Moses blessed the people 233 years later, however, the individual tribes had evolved. Now each tribe, with one exception, was equal to the others in status, and it was no longer necessary to treat the four "lesser" tribes differently. Moreover, on the threshold of entering the land, the Jewish people had agreed to a compact whereby each individual tribe took responsibility for all the others. Moses memorialized this intertwined fate by narrowing the gaps between the blessings to the tribes.

The one exception was the tribe of Yehudah, whose blessing is followed by a larger *pesuchah* gap. Following the conquest of the Northern Kingdom about 2,700 years ago, the tribe of Yehudah represented the majority of the Jewish nation. Perhaps Moses' placement of a larger *pesuchah* gap after the blessing to Yehudah reflected his Divinely inspired intuition that Yehudah was the one tribe that could exist independently if necessary and be the surviving remnant from which the eternal nation would continue.

ii. One Year Short

MOSES' BLESSING TO THE TRIBE OF BENJAMIN OBLIQUELY refers to both Temples, which were destined to be located in his territory (33:12). "Of Benjamin, he said: 'May God's beloved dwell securely by Him, He hovers over him all day long, and rests between his shoulders.'" Prior to the construction of the Temple, located in the land of Benjamin, the permanent structure of the Tabernacle had been located in Shiloh, which is in the territory of Ephraim, Joseph's son.

Jacob had only two sons from his more beloved wife Rachel — Joseph and Benjamin. During her lifetime, Jacob's main residence was in her tent. As a continuation of this model, the metaphorical central tent of the entire Jewish people was established in the inheritance of her offspring, the lands of Benjamin and Joseph.

The Talmud (*Zevachim* 118b) states that the Tabernacle at Shiloh, the First Temple and the Second endured for 369, 410 and 420 years respectively. The sum of all three is 1,199 years, just shy of 1,200.

In a different context, the Maharal contends that the number 12 relates to the concept of giving full expression to a thing or idea. Thus, 12 vertices define the space of a cube, the quintessential three-dimensional space. Appropriate to this, the numerical value of the word for "this" (*zeh*), a definite article, is 12. The Jewish people find their complete expression through 12 tribes. Furthermore, our Sages interpret the word *zeh*, as it appears a number of places in the Torah, as an indication that God actually showed Moses the item in question. For example, the Torah introduces nonkosher animals with the word "this," and our Sages infer that God actually showed Moses the various nonkosher animals so he could differentiate them from the kosher ones. Here, too, 12 indicates setting the precise and definite parameters of a thing.

Perhaps it can be suggested that this total number of almost but not quite 1,200 years of the three Divine Abodes reflects the historic failure of the Jewish people to facilitate the complete expression of God's presence among men. Their best year still awaits them.

iii. The Odor of Bad Deeds

THE TORAH RELATES THAT GOD DID NOT ALLOW MOSES TO enter the land of Israel (34:4). "And God to [Moses], 'This is the land that I swore to give to Abraham, to Isaac and to Jacob, saying, "I will give it to your offspring"; I have let you see with your own eyes, but you shall not cross over to there.'" Moses, like many of our ancestors, awaits the coming of the Messiah and the resurrection of the dead to enter the land.

The Talmud (*Berachos* 24b) records that Rav Abba wished to relocate from Babylon to the land of Israel, but Rav Yehudah, his teacher, was against the idea, basing his position on the words of the prophet (*Jeremiah* 27), "'They shall come to Babylon and remain there until the day I redeem them,' says God." According to Rav Yehudah's reading, the verse restricts Jews from returning to live in Israel during the period of the exile, probably in order to induce us to repent and gain an eventual complete return (*geulah sheleimah*).

The Talmud goes on to relate that Rav Abba decided to slip away to Israel without announcing his departure to his teacher, but not before attending one last lecture. That day, Rav Yehudah taught that if someone breaks wind while praying he must interrupt his prayer until the vile odor dissipates and only then resume praying. Upon hearing these words, Rav Abba declared, "Had I come today only to hear this ruling, it would have been worthwhile."

It seems from the story that Rav Abba expressed an added satisfaction in hearing this particular law. Why was this so?

Rav Abba may have felt some reservations about leaving surreptitiously for Israel without Rav Yehudah's approval. And then he heard Rav Yehudah's ruling, and it reassured him; he discerned in it a providential hint, a message specifically for him. Rav Yehudah had said that one may resume praying once the foul odor passes. Rav Abba drew an analogy. Just as prayer is legally construed as standing before God, so too is living in Israel the equivalent of living before God. Consequently, just as one may resume praying once the foul odor passes, so too may one return to the land of Israel during the period of the exile once the stench of the misdeeds that led to the destruction of the Temple and our exile have passed. Rav Abba understood this to mean that he was correct in his decision.

iv. *Bread Without Shame*

THE TORAH ENDS WITH GOD PERFORMING AN ACT OF KINDness (34:6). "And He buried [Moses] in the cleft." The Talmud (*Sotah* 14b) observes that the Torah also begins with God performing an act of kindness (3:21), "And God the Lord made for man and his wife a garment of skin and dressed them."

The similarity between beginning and end extends beyond mere acts of kindness. In both instances, God's kindness is to clothe man. He dresses Adam and Eve, and He covers Moses' forlorn and inanimate body with earth, dressing it in its final garb. Clothing provides dignity, covering man's shame. In fact, the root of the word clothe is comprised of two syllables, the first of which is a *lamed* (ל) meaning "for," and the second is *beis shin* (בש),

meaning "shame"; the purpose of the clothing is "for shame," to remove it.

The awfulness of shame is an essential concept in creation. The *Zohar* explains that since unearned benefit is considered *nahama d'kesufa*, the bread of shame, God created a world in which man could earn reward by exercising his free will.

The Psalmist declares (89:3), "The world is built through kindness (*olam chessed yibaneh*)." Perhaps more correctly translated, "Eternity will be built with kindness." God's kindness continually suffuses all of creation. Through its study and observance, the corpus of the entire Torah — the beginning, the end and everything in between — reflects God's ultimate act of kindness, the metaphysical clothing God bestows on man to protect him from shame.

Epilogue

Let Us Return

I CONCLUDE THIS LABOR OF SEVERAL YEARS WITH A BRIEF vignette. Some time ago, I was sitting in a dentist's chair, chatting with the dentist about a tractate he had been studying for several years. He said he would soon be completing the entire tractate, and I congratulated him. I asked him if he intended to make an elaborate *siyum*, a celebratory meal for friends and family in honor of the occasion. "I don't think so," he replied somewhat sheepishly. "I know I should, but I just feel uncomfortable doing it. It's almost like boasting, isn't it?" My first thought was to argue with the good doctor, but the drill in my mouth gave me pause.

Afterwards, I began to wonder. Why indeed should we be proud of the completion of a unit of Torah study? Is our accomplishment any more than a drop in the infinite ocean of Torah knowledge? Compared to the infinite expanse of the Torah, the infinitesimal fractions we acquire in our lifetimes, even under the best of circumstances, are the mathematical equivalent of zero. Why then did our Sages encourage a festive meal and establish a special *Kaddish* upon the completion of a unit of Torah study?

The answer lies in the preface to the special *Kaddish* recited upon the completion of a unit of Torah study. Its two essential themes are a statement of appreciation to God for having given us the ability to study Torah and a prayer for continued opportunities to do so. We refer to the entire piece by its first word, *Hadran*, which means "let us return." The word occurs as part of our supplication for continued opportunity to study God's infinite wisdom. We may deduce from this that our joy and celebration is not over accomplishment, but rather over a certain measure of opportunity to delve into God's infinite wisdom.

I close this work with my own *Hadran*. I am grateful to God for allowing me to peer into His infinite wisdom, and I beseech Him for further opportunities to probe and expound His holy Torah.

Glossary

Amidah: The thrice daily central prayer, also known as the *Shemoneh Esrei,* the Eighteen Blessings

chessed: kindness

hakaras hatov: appreciation

Kohen (Kohanim): priest(s)

Kohein Gadol: High Priest

lashon hara: gossip, slander, or evil speech

Mishkan: Tabernacle; place of centralized worship

parashah: the weekly Torah portion; by tradition, the five Books of the Torah are divided into fifty-four *parshios*

pesuchah: a gap in the Torah scroll that leaves blank the remainder of the line on which a verse ends

stumah: a gap in the Torah scroll equivalent to four letter-sized blank spaces

yetzer hara: the evil inclination; the aspect of man that encourages him to act improperly, creating the opportunity for free will

Selected Bibliography

Maharal

Acronym of R' Yehudah Loewe ben Bezalel, of Prague.

(c. 1512-1609)

One of the seminal figures in the last 500 years of Jewish thought, Rav Yehudah was born c. 1512 and died in Prague in 1609. His genealogy can be traced to King David.

Although he was universally acknowledged as one of the rabbinic greats of the era, while his life was not an easy one. He delayed his marriage fro 20 years due to financial difficulties. He was Chief Rabbi of Moravia, residing in Nikolsburg, for 20 years. Then, in 1573, he transferred his yeshiva to Prague, the Torah metropolis of Europe. Upon two different occasions, he accepted the rabbinate of Posen in order to settle communal strife.

He was elected Chief Rabbi of Prague in 1597 as a very old man. It appears that the position had been denied him up to then because of his outspokenness in attacking social evils and religious laxity.

Though commonly known as a folk hero and miracle worker, his greatest contribution was his formulation of a self-contained system of Jewish thought. His many books and lengthy sermons formed the basis for much of the significant writing of succeeding centuries.

Among his many erudite works were: *Novellae* on *Shulchan Aruch Yoreh Deah; Gur Aryeh* on the Torah; *Be'er haGolah* on the *Passover Hagaddah; Derech Chaim; Netzach Yisrael; Nesivos Olam, etc.*

Malbim

Acronym of Meir Leibush ben Yechiel Michel.

(1809-1879)

Rav, preacher and Biblical commentator.

The Malbim was also known as the '*ilui* [prodigy] from Volhynia.' He was Rav in several cities, but he suffered much persecution on account of his uncompromising and stand against Reform, leading to his short-term imprisonment on a false accusation. He wandered much of his life, serving as Rav in various cities for several years at a time.

His fame and immense popularity rests upon his commentary to the Bible which was widely esteemed. His first published commentary was on *Megillas Esther* (1845). His commentary to the remaining books of the Bible were published between then and 1876.

Rambam

Acronym of R' Moshe ben Maimon; Maimonides.

(1135-1204).

One of the most illustrious figures in Judaism in the post-Talmudic era, and among the greatest of all time. He was a rabbinic authority, codifier, philosopher, and royal physician. According to some, he was a descendant of Rav Yehudah haNasi.

Born in Cordoba; Moved to Eretz Yisrael and then to Fostat, the old city of Cairo, Egypt.

At the age of 23 he began his commentary on the *Mishnah*, which he authored all through his wanderings. His main work was *Mishneh-Torah Yad-haChazakah*, his codification of the spectrum of Halachah until this day. This was the only book he wrote in Hebrew, all his other works having been written in Arabic, a fact he regretted later in his life.

He is also known for his *Moreh Nevuchim ('Guide for the Perplexed')*, and for his many works in the field of medicine, hygiene, astronomy, etc.

Ramban

Acronym of R' Moshe ben Nachman; Nachmanides.

(1194-1270)

One of the leading Torah scholars and authors of Talmudic literature during the generation following Rambam; also a renowned philosopher, biblical commentator, poet and physician.

Born in Gerona, to a famous rabbinic family. He is sometimes referred to, after his native town, as Rabbenu Moshe Gerondi, where he spent most of his life, supporting himself as a physician. He exercised extensive influence over Jewish life. Even King James I consulted him on occasion.

Already at the age of 16 he had published works on Talmud and Halachah.

Among his works were: *Milchemes Hashem*, in defense of the Rif against the '*hasagos*' of Rav Zerachiah haLevi in *Sefer haMaor*; *Sefer haZechus*, in response to the '*hasagos*' of the Ravad on the Rif; *Sefer haMitzvos; Iggeres HaRamban; Iggeres hakodesh*; and his profound and encyclopedic Commentary on the Torah, which is printed in all large editions of the Bible.

In 1263 he was coerced by King James I into holding a public disputation with the apostate Pablo Christiani. The Ramban's victory aroused the anger of the church and resulted in his barely succeeding to escape from Spain. He then emigrated to Eretz Yisrael. In 1268 he became Rav in Acco, successor to Rav Yechiel of Paris.

He died in 1276.

Rashi

Acronym of R' Shlomo Yitzchaki

(1040-1105)

Leading commentator on the Bible and Talmud.

He was born in Troyes, France in 1040 – the year in which Rabbeinu Gershom Maor haGolah died. According to tradition, Rashi's ancestry goes back to Rav Yochanan haSandlar and to King David.

The summit of Rashi's commentaries was his commentary on the Talmud – an encyclopedic and brilliant undertaking. Nothing can be compared to the impact this commentary had had upon all who study the Talmud. Rashi's commentary has opened to all what otherwise would have been a sealed book. Without his commentary, no one would dare navigate the 'Sea of Talmud.' Every word is precise and laden wit inner meaning. Rashi's corrections of the Talmud text were, for the most part, introduced into the standard editions and became the accepted text.

Rashi's Commentary to the Bible, too, made a similar impact – and virtually every printed Bible contains his commentary, which is distinguished by its conciseness and clarity.

Many Halachic works from the 'School of Rashi' have come down to us: *Sefer haOrah; Sefer haPardes; Machzor Vitry; Siddur Rashi;* and responsa.

Rashi died on Tammuz 29, 1105.